Response to *Radical* and *Radical Together*

"I love this book! Please read it. God is using David Platt to lead his church into much-needed reform. *Radical Together* is filled with tremendous insight from a man who loves Christ's church. I don't know of a church leader that I trust more."

—FRANCIS CHAN, best-selling author of *Crazy Love*

"I have the privilege of knowing David Platt, and I assure you that his life and ministry commend what he has written here. Read *Radical Together*. Like the right medicine, it may be more helpful than comfortable. In fact, my prayer is that it may be an explosion, shifting many churches from centering wrongly on ourselves to centering rightly on Christ and his agenda for us—and for his world."

—MARK DEVER, senior pastor, Capitol Hill Baptist Church,
Washington DC

"*Radical* caused many Christians to be shaken and to reevaluate their lives. *Radical Together* will do the same for our churches. *Radical Together* is such a clarion call for churches across the world to follow the clear teachings of the Word that I began to pray that this book would indeed move thousands of churches to become biblically radical. Many churches and Christians will never be the same again after reading the book and following its biblical precepts."

—THOM S. RAINER, president and CEO, LifeWay Christian
Resources, and coauthor of *The Millennials* and *Simple Church*

"Platt's arguments…emerge at a post-excess moment, when attitude toward material life are up for grabs. His book has struck a chord."

—DAVID BROOKS, *The New York Times*

"Full of spiritual pronouncements readers of any religion can appreciate…*Radical* caters mostly to Christians, as a fervent manual to the faithful. If you're stuck in the American dream of 'self-advancement, self-esteem, and self-sufficiency,' as Platt describes it, then the book could be a good fit for you, too."

—SPENCER BAILEY, *TheDailyBeast.com*

"What's significant about Platt's perspective is that it is coming from a solidly conservative voice in the evangelical mainstream."

—JONATHAN MERRITT, *The Huffington Post*

"This book is a challenge for Christians to wake up, trade in their false 'American dreams,' and live a Christ-centered life."

—JAY PERONI, CFP, *Crosswalk.com*

"David's honesty and wide range of experiences make him an accessible and engaging author… There is much to like about *Radical*. I applaud David's call for serious discipleship."

—KEVIN DEYOUNG, The Gospel Coalition

"[Platt is] biblical, straightforward, brutally honest, and writes a powerful narrative as he sets out to discover what Jesus really taught to first century followers."

—MATTHEW ROBBINS, *TheChristianManifesto.com*

"David Platt challenges Christians to wake up, trade in false values rooted in the American dream, and embrace the notion that each of us is blessed by God for a global purpose—to make Christ's glory known to all the nations! This is a must-read for every believer!"

—WESS STAFFORD, president and CEO, Compassion International

UNLEASHING THE PEOPLE OF GOD
FOR THE PURPOSE OF GOD

RADICAL
TOGETHER

DAVID
PLATT

MULTNOMAH
BOOKS

RADICAL TOGETHER
PUBLISHED BY MULTNOMAH BOOKS
12265 Oracle Boulevard, Suite 200
Colorado Springs, Colorado 80921

All Scripture quotations, unless otherwise indicated, are taken from the Holy Bible, New International Version®, NIV®. Copyright © 1973, 1978, 1984 by Biblica Inc.™ Used by permission of Zondervan. All rights reserved worldwide. www.zondervan.com. Scripture quotations marked (KJV) are taken from the King James Version.

Details in some anecdotes and stories have been changed to protect the identities of the persons involved.

ISBN 978-1-60142-372-6
ISBN 978-1-60142-373-3 (electronic)

Copyright © 2011 by David Platt

Cover design by Mark D. Ford.

Published in association with Yates & Yates, LLP, Attorneys and Counselors, Orange, California.

The author's royalties from this book will go toward promoting the glory of Christ in all nations.

All rights reserved. No part of this book may be reproduced or transmitted in any form or by any means, electronic or mechanical, including photocopying and recording, or by any information storage and retrieval system, without permission in writing from the publisher.

Published in the United States by WaterBrook Multnomah, an imprint of the Crown Publishing Group, a division of Random House Inc., New York.

MULTNOMAH and its mountain colophon are registered trademarks of Random House Inc.

Library of Congress Cataloging-in-Publication Data
Platt, David.
    Radical together : unleashing the people of God for the purpose of God / David Platt.
        p. cm.
    Includes bibliographical references (p.   ).
    ISBN 978-1-60142-372-6 — ISBN 978-1-60142-373-3 (electronic)
    1. Church. I. Title.
    BV600.3.P63 2011
    250—dc22

                                2011001781

Printed in the United States of America
2011

10 9 8 7 6 5 4 3 2

SPECIAL SALES
Most WaterBrook Multnomah books are available at special quantity discounts when purchased in bulk by corporations, organizations, and special-interest groups. Custom imprinting or excerpting can also be done to fit special needs. For information, please e-mail SpecialMarkets@WaterBrookMultnomah.com or call 1-800-603-7051.

To the Church at Brook Hills,
"whom I love and long for, my joy and crown."
—Philippians 4:1

CONTENTS

INTRODUCTION

High atop the Andes Mountains, the rays of the sun strike ice, and a single drop of water forms. It begins to trace a hesitant course downward, gradually joining with other drops of water to become a steady stream. The stream gains speed and strength. Thousands of feet below and hundreds of miles later, what were once single drops have converged to become the mightiest river on earth: the Amazon. Flowing into the Atlantic Ocean at a rate of more than seven million cubic feet per second, the Amazon is more powerful than the next ten largest rivers in the world combined.

In my first book, *Radical*, I explored how the biblical gospel affects individual Christian lives. Simply put, in a world of urgent spiritual and physical need, gospel-believing, God-exalting men and women do not have time to waste their lives pursuing a Christian spin on the American dream. Using the imagery above, I tried to picture what happens when the truth of Christ penetrates our hearts, melts our assumptions, and propels us on a journey of abandonment to God.

But you and I are not intended to plunge down the mountain

of radical obedience alone. That's one of the reasons I love this imagery of the Amazon. The force of a single drop of water descending the Andes is minuscule. Similarly, as long as individual Christians journey alone—no matter how "radical" they are—their effect will be minimal. But as men and women who are surrendered to the person of Christ join together in churches that are committed to the purpose of Christ, then nothing can stop the spread of the gospel to the ends of the earth.

In *Radical Together,* I want to consider what happens—or can happen—when we apply the revolutionary claims and commands of Christ to our communities of faith. I want to contemplate the force of a people who come together to enjoy God's grace in the church while they extend God's glory in the world. And I want to propose that a movement of such people in such churches has the potential to permeate nations with the praise of God.

I am speaking to believers who are ready to lead, influence, or simply be a part of such a movement in their local church. You may be a follower of Christ who desires to live out a more biblical gospel, and you want to see your church do the same. You may be a pastor, staff person, or leader of some other description in the church, and you want your local fellowship to count for the spread of God's glory in the world. You may even be a Christian who is tempted to throw in the towel and say, "My church will never be radical."

Whatever your circumstance, in this book I invite you to engage God's Word and God's world with a fresh, honest, and open perspective so that together we might answer one question:

How can we in the church best unleash the people of God
in the Spirit of God with the Word of God
for the glory of God in the world?

As I pose this question, I do not claim to be an expert on how to answer it. I am merely one pastor in one church, and I have so much to learn. Yet I know that, as leaders and members of churches, we are called to spur one another toward Christ and his agenda in the world. And I am convinced that in the church we can—unknowingly and unintentionally—actually prevent God's people from accomplishing God's purpose. If we are not careful, our activities in the church can hinder the advancement of Christ's kingdom. For this reason I believe certain ideas are foundational for Christians who desire to be a part of churches that are unleashing people into the world with the gospel.

This book is organized around six such ideas. I do not claim they are exhaustive, but as a pastor working out the implications of the gospel in a local church, I do believe these ideas are essential. Here's a preview:

1. One of the worst enemies of Christians can be good things in the church.
2. The gospel that saves us from work saves us to work.
3. The Word does the work.
4. Building the right church depends on using all the wrong people.
5. We are living—and longing—for the end of the world.
6. We are selfless followers of a self-centered God.

At first glance these ideas may seem fanciful, even untrue. I understand that. But then many of Jesus' statements struck his listeners that way too. Statements like these: "Many who are first will be last, and many who are last will be first," "For he who is least among you all—he is the greatest," and "Whoever finds his life will lose it, and whoever loses his life for my sake will find it."[1] Though I certainly don't claim the authority or creativity of Jesus, my aim is to put forward ideas that at first may seem confusing, if not contradictory, but upon deeper investigation will bring to light important realities that most overlook.

I hope and pray that accurate theological foundations undergird all my practical exhortations. I am grateful for valuable resources that help us understand the nature and marks of the church.[2] But I want to be clear that my goal here is not to present a comprehensive overview of the church. Instead, it is to build upon biblical foundations in order to consider practical implications for how a right understanding of the church fuels radical obedience among Christians.

Throughout the history of humankind, God has chosen to call out not just individuals but a people for himself. He told the Israelites, "I will walk among you and be your God, and you will be my people." Through Christ, God brought Jews and Gentiles together as "one body" in which "each member belongs to all the others." Peter told the church, "You are a chosen people,…a people belonging to God, that you may declare the praises of him who called you out of darkness into his wonderful light." Indeed, God's intention is that "through the church, the manifold wisdom of God should be made known to the rulers and authorities in the heavenly realms."[3]

If you and I want our lives to count for God's purpose in the world, we need to begin with a commitment to God's people in the church. God has called us to lock arms with one another in single-minded, death-defying obedience to one objective: the declaration of his gospel for the demonstration of his glory to all nations. This is God's design for his people, and it is worth giving our lives to see it accomplished. It is worth it for billions of people who do not yet know that Jesus is the grave-conquering, life-giving, all-satisfying King. And it is worth it for you and me, because we were made to enjoy the great pleasures of God in the context of total abandonment to his global purpose.

CHAPTER ONE

TYRANNY
OF THE GOOD

ONE OF THE WORST ENEMIES OF CHRISTIANS CAN BE GOOD THINGS IN THE CHURCH.

Before Mark came to the Church at Brook Hills (the church I serve), he had spent practically his entire adult life involved in church programs and serving on church committees. "You name it, and I did it," Mark said. "I was on finance teams and personnel teams. I worked on capital building campaigns and sat in long-term planning sessions. Every week my schedule was filled with church activity."

After becoming a part of our faith family, Mark started hearing people talk about making disciples. That's when he realized that, despite all the good things he had done in the church, he could not name one person outside his family whom he had led to Christ and who was now walking with Christ and leading others to Christ. Mark said to me, "David, I have spent my life doing all the stuff in the church that I thought I was supposed to do.

But I'm realizing that I have missed the most important thing: making disciples." At his workplace and in our community, Mark is now intentionally leading people to Christ and teaching them to follow him.

The story of Mark's life as a Christian should frighten us. The last thing you and I want to do is waste our lives on religious activity that is devoid of spiritual productivity—being active in the church but not advancing the kingdom of God. We don't want to come to the end of our days on earth only to realize that we have had little impact on more people going to heaven. Yet if we are not careful, we will spend our lives doing good things in the church while we ultimately miss out on the great purpose for which we were created.

That's why I say one of the worst enemies of Christians can be good things in the church.

Of course, some will disagree with my claim. "How can good things in the church really be one of our worst enemies?" some might ask. "Sin and Satan are our worst enemies," they might say. And they would have a point. But let me point something out: We *know* sin and Satan are our enemies. We *know* we need to be on our guard against them. But too often we're oblivious to the threat posed by the good things we're doing. We've laid down our defenses against the way that the *good* can hinder the *best.* In this sense, good things can subtly and effectively become one of our worst enemies.

As Christians today, you and I can easily deceive ourselves into thinking that dedication to church programs automatically equals devotion to kingdom purposes. We can fill our lives and our churches with *good* things requiring our resources and *good* activities demanding our attention that are not ultimately *best* for the enjoyment of the gospel in our churches and the spread of the gospel in our communities.

We must be willing to sacrifice good things in the church in order to experience the great things of God.

PUTTING EVERYTHING ON THE TABLE

For this reason I propose that we must put everything on the table. We have to put everything, even good things in the church, up for reconsideration before God, releasing them wholly to him and asking him to show us his priorities and purposes for each.

I'm not talking about biblical essentials and theological non-negotiables. As we will see soon enough, we do not need to change the words of God or the truths of the gospel. To do so would be foolish and fatal.

But everything else belongs on the table. The ways we minister to children, youth, and college students; how we serve women, men, singles, marrieds, and seniors; how we do music and mission; how we approach and implement finances and budgets, administration and communication; all our policies, priorities, and procedures; all the buildings and land we own or rent—all these things (and more) belong on the table. The gospel compels the church to go to God with everything we have and everything we do and then ask, "What needs to go? What needs to change? What needs to stay the same?"

And then wait for God to answer.

Why wouldn't this be what the gospel demands? After all, we follow a Savior who said things like "Any of you who does not give up everything he has cannot be my disciple" and "If anyone would come after me, he must deny himself and take up his cross daily and follow me."[1] A church is a community of individuals who have lost their lives to follow Christ. Surely it flows from this that we would be willing to lose our programs and our preferences, to sacrifice our budgets and our buildings, to let go of our most cherished legacies and reputations if there is a better way to make his glory known in the world.

BREACHED LEVEES AND OVERTURNED LIVES

I will not soon forget the day in August 2005 when my wife, Heather, and I fled New Orleans. It was the day before Hurricane Katrina struck. We were used to hurricane warnings, and it was common to leave the city for a couple of days and then return. So we grabbed some extra clothes, hopped in the car, and drove out of town. Little did we know that this would be the last time we would see our house—and our neighborhood—in the same condition.

Two days later we were serving at an evacuation shelter. We had set up a projector and a screen so people could see the news coming in from the city. After we had arranged everything, we sat down to watch the live feeds. That's when we saw it. As the news helicopter flew over one drowned neighborhood after another, we suddenly recognized the gas station (or what used to be a gas station) just a couple of blocks from our house. As the camera continued to pan across the lakelike landscape, we saw our neighborhood engulfed in water up to the rooftops. And then we glimpsed a rooftop we thought was ours…

We sat in stunned silence, our thoughts racing. Home for us had just been swept away.

When we took walks around that house in the early evening, we'd wander up to the levee a couple of blocks away. The levee was one of many structures designed to protect the city from the water surrounding it. Thick walls of steel and concrete driven deep into the ground defined the boundaries of Lake Pontchartrain, the Mississippi River, and ultimately the Gulf of Mexico.

But as the floodwaters rose, the walls began to crack. The levee started splitting—at first a little at a time, but then more and more until finally the barricade broke, and millions of gallons of water came rushing out. One of our neighbor's homes was picked up by the force of the flood and carried down the street. Before long, our entire neighborhood, including our house, was submerged.

Like others who lost everything in the flood, Heather and I experienced shock and disbelief. Then we felt confused. In the days that followed, we talked and we prayed and we wondered when "normal" was going to return.

But now we see it in a new light altogether.

For us, the flood depicts the radical call of Christ to Christians and the church. When Jesus calls us to abandon everything we have and everything we are, it's almost as if he is daring us to put ourselves in the flood plain. To put all our lives and all our churches, all our property and all our possessions, all our plans and all our strategies, all our hopes and all our dreams in front of the levee and then to ask God to break it. To ask God to sweep away whatever he wants, to leave standing whatever he desires, and to remake our lives and churches according to his will.

THE HEART OF THE QUESTION

Let me ask: Are you there personally? Is your church?

Specifically, is your community of faith willing to put everything down before God and say, "We will do whatever you want, we will drop whatever you command, we will eliminate whatever is not best, and we will add whatever is necessary in order to make your glory known in the world around us, no matter what it costs us"?

I remember one of the first meetings I had with the leaders at Brook Hills after becoming their pastor. We were talking about the future of the church, and I began with a list of questions:

- How can we most effectively mobilize the people of this church to accomplish the Great Commission?
- How can we most effectively organize the leadership of this church to accomplish the Great Commission?
- Do we need all the staff, teams, and committees we have?
- Does our church budget reflect the desires and design of God in his Word?
- Are our multimillion-dollar facilities the best use of our money for the accomplishment of God's purposes in the world?

- Are all the programs we have created the absolute best way to advance the gospel from our community to the ends of the earth?
- What good things do we have or what good things are we doing that we need to abolish or alter for greater ends?

When you ask questions like these, people wonder if you're looking for a short tenure as pastor.

That night at Brook Hills, folks responded to my questions with thoughtful questions of their own. "What does this mean for us, Pastor?" "What positions do you think are unnecessary in our leadership structure?" "Are you saying we need to sell the building?" "What programs are you suggesting we alter or abolish?"

I remember well some of the ensuing discussions. We talked about various programs and activities in the church, and it was not uncommon to hear the question, "Well, what's wrong with doing these things?" One person would ask, "What's wrong with having a fall carnival for children?" Another would ask, "What's wrong with having a basketball league?"

We all quickly realized, though, that asking what's wrong with certain programs and activities would get us nowhere. No one was going to say that children having fun at a carnival or people playing basketball was a bad thing. The conversation would change only when we asked, "Are these programs and activities the *best* way to spend our time, money, and energy for the spread of the gospel in our neighborhood and in all nations?"

All of a sudden we found ourselves open to letting go of good things in order to achieve greater purposes. Our perspective had radically changed.

Now, that didn't make it easy to let go of good things. To be honest, we have not always done a good job of letting good things go. Sometimes we have moved too quickly or too slowly. Sometimes our communication about change has been confusing at best. As a result, some have left the church, and I grieve over any unnecessary thing I have done to cause that. At Brook Hills we have learned that letting go of good things is one of the hardest things to do in the church.

But even as we talked together on that first night, we realized we didn't have to answer every question immediately. None of us, including me, had answers to all the questions, and we still don't. The key is simply to ask the questions. For in honestly asking, we begin to grasp how much the good things in the church have a hold on our hearts.

We begin to discover our dangerous tendency to value our traditions over God's truth, just as Jesus warned.[2] We find ourselves defending a program because that's what worked before, not because that's what God has said to do now. We realize how prone we are to exalt our work over God's will, our dreams over God's desires, and our plans over God's priorities.

We see up close a propensity in our budgets to value our comforts over others' needs. As I write this, more than five hundred million people in the world are starving to death. They lack food, water, and basic medical care. Children are dying of diseases like diarrhea; many who live will suffer lifelong brain damage from early protein deficiency. Others will be sold into forced labor or trafficked for sexual exploitation. Nearly one hundred fifty million children are orphans. Yet judging by what we hang on to in our churches, convenient programs and nice parking lots are still more important than such children and their families.

One pastor who contacted me recently was upset about *Radical*. His church was starting a multimillion-dollar building campaign, and some of his members who had read the book were expressing hesitancy about moving forward. I told him—as I would tell any other pastor—that my goal is not to incite division. I obviously cannot claim to know what a church should do in every situation. I simply and humbly want to ask the question, "Amid all the good things we are doing and planning, are there better ways to align with God's Word, mobilize God's people, and marshal God's resources for God's glory in a world where millions of people are starving and more than a billion have never even heard of Jesus?"

Some would say that's not a fair question. I'm convinced it is a question we cannot avoid.

CHANGING FOCUS

My conversation with our team at Brook Hills that night led us down a road of continually rethinking our use of resources. Yet I found myself longing for a catalyst to spur us toward a more sweeping reprioritization of our time and money.

During the fall of 2009, we were studying the book of James as a church. (Warning: don't engage honestly with the book of

James unless you are ready to put everything on the table!) When we came to James 2, we were confronted with the reality that those who have received mercy extend mercy. Grace in our hearts overflows in goodness from our hands. James makes it clear that people who claim to be Christians but who fail to help poverty-stricken fellow believers are in fact not saved.[3] It's not that acts of mercy are a *means to* salvation, but they are clear *evidence of* salvation. (For more on this, see chapter 2.)

At the same time we were studying James, we were going through our church budgeting process. To be honest, I hate budget season. As a pastor, I believe that is when the church comes face to face with how prone we are to give our resources to good things while ignoring great need. Christians in North America give, on average, 2.5 percent of their income to their church. Out of that 2.5 percent, churches in North America will give 2 percent of their budgeted monies to needs overseas.[4] In other words, for every one hundred dollars a North American Christian earns, he will give five cents through the church to a world with urgent spiritual and physical needs. This does not make sense.

Knowing this, one night our pastors took a hard look at the realities of the world, from the vast numbers of our brothers and sisters who are starving to the great multitudes who have never heard the gospel. Then we looked at our budget. And then we took action. We decided to drastically change our spending to better align with the will and ways of God.

This began with reallocating budget overages. Our staff had already been frugal, and we had saved more than $500,000 for the future. But James caused us to realize that we had brothers and sisters around the world who already needed it. So we decided to give it all away—specifically through partnerships with churches in India, where 41 percent of the world's poor live.

Then we began looking at our 2010 budget. We decided to ask the staff to go through the budget with a fine-tooth comb and cut every expenditure possible so we could give more around the world. When I sat down with our leaders, I tried to soften the blow of what cuts might mean for individual ministries. But as I was sharing, one of our preschool leaders spoke up. "David," she said, "you don't have to go soft on us. We realize from God's Word that this is something we need to do, and it is something we want to do. So let us get to work and start cutting our budgets!"

With that said, we split into different teams to reevaluate our budgets. What happened next was amazing. Whereas the budgeting process usually involves leaders vying with one another to see who can raise their budget the most, this year our leaders were competing with one another to see who could cut their budget the most.

There were big cuts—our worship ministry leaders sliced 83 percent from their budget. And there were little cuts. For example, preschool leaders looked at every detail in their budget, including snacks. They reasoned that the kids on Sunday morning have a great breakfast and a great lunch, so why do they need a full assortment of snacks in between? They decided to simplify the snacks and save hundreds of dollars.

One Sunday some weeks later, I was driving home from Brook Hills with my family, and I asked my then-three-year-old son, "How was your time at Brook Hills today, buddy?"

Looking downcast, he replied, "We didn't have any Goldfish today, Daddy."

After a short pause my wife chimed in. "You know, that is your daddy's fault, Son!"

I didn't know whether to laugh or hide. But that's when it came home to me that these changes wouldn't affect just the leadership in the church. They would affect the entire church—all the way down to the preschoolers.

Others were seeing the same thing. So we believed it was important to have the entire church vote on moving forward in this direction, and that's what we did. We put a proposal before our church family that said:

In love to God, in light of the needs around the world, and in obedience to Scripture (Proverbs 14:31; 21:13; 28:27; Matthew 25:31–46; James 2:14–17; 1 John 3:16–18), the leadership of the Church at Brook Hills proposes that the church body affirm the following actions:

- We will immediately begin radical saving as a church during the remainder of 2009 for the sake of urgent spiritual and physical need around the world.

- Our leadership will work together over the next two months on a 2010 budget that saves every expenditure possible for the sake of urgent spiritual and physical need around the world.

- We will immediately designate up to $525,000 of our current excess cash to serve impoverished churches across India.

A couple of weeks later, the church voted overwhelmingly in favor of reallocating resources in this direction. We were able to free up an additional $1.5 million from our 2010 church budget. With that money we began to focus more on spreading the gospel in Birmingham and around the world.

Locally, we identified an area of our city with particular needs, and we committed time and money to partner with other churches, organizations, and schools to share and show the gospel in tangible ways there. Not wanting to give our money without going ourselves, we challenged every member in our faith family to pray about leaving their comfortable neighborhoods and moving into this area of the city. Since that time, several individuals, couples, and families have done exactly that.

Globally, we focused on northern India, home to six hundred million people, but fewer than 0.5 percent are evangelical Christians. Based on relationships we already had and new partnerships we were able to form, we committed time and money to meeting urgent needs there. During the year, through local Indian churches, we were able to provide food, education, medical care, and, most important, the gospel to more than a thousand families in unreached and extremely impoverished areas. In addition, we were able to work with other Indian churches to build a hundred wells that would provide clean water for tens of thousands who previously didn't have it. On top of these things, we were able to train hundreds of national church leaders, mobilize church planters to engage hundreds of villages for the first time with the good news of Christ, and give millions access to the Bible in their language for the first time.

My purpose in sharing these things is not to draw attention to our church. Anything we have done is merely evidence of God's grace among us. And we know we have a long way to go. I share these things simply to encourage you to consider the possibilities of what might happen when churches decide to put everything on the table and spend our resources intentionally and sacrificially for the glory of our King.

DOWNSIZING FOR A GREATER VISION

As you read the numbers I just mentioned, you might have been thinking, *Well, not many churches have $500,000 just lying around. And not every church is able to give $1.5 million away!*

But this is the beauty of God's plan. You don't have to possess a certain amount of resources in order to spend it wisely for the glory of God. Every church and every Christian has good resources that can be used for great purposes.

One student minister in a smaller church e-mailed me to share what God was doing in his fellowship.

> We have already found about $15,000 in our budget that we are going to reallocate to things like: (1) a gospel-centered organization that helps impoverished children around the world; (2) a foundation that will enable 40,000 people to be parasite-free for an entire year (parasites kill more people than cancer in third-world countries); (3) encouraging families in our church to adopt by offering scholarships to cover the costs of adoption; and

(4) adding $3,000 to our mission scholarship fund to enable even more youth to go on a mission trip this summer. In addition, we believe that next year we will be able to redirect even more of our operating budget to needs like these here and around the world.

It doesn't take a big budget to have a large impact. All it takes is a family budget, for that matter. I received another e-mail from a dad who is currently deployed overseas in the armed forces. His wife read *Radical* and told him he needed to read it. He was able to find only about seventy pages of the book online (which didn't even include the chapter on giving), but he told me how the words from Scripture that I referenced had penetrated his heart. Here's the way he described what happened next:

> I grew up in the church, and my wife and I attend and give our tithe, but I have neglected the relationship Jesus calls us to. I feel sick about the way I have been living my life, in pursuit of the American dream, living to lift myself up! So about six days ago, my wife and I (over the phone) decided to start selling our worthless possessions. In the last five days, we sold two TVs, an iPhone, a computer, a TV stand, some curtains, and our new car. We also made a commitment to start the adoption process when I get home and hopefully add to the four boys God has already blessed us with.
>
> We had bought our car new five months ago, and I just knew we were going to take at least a $5,000 hit on it.

When my wife took the car in to the dealership to see
what the damage would be, we weren't surprised to hear
them quote a price about $6,000 less than what we owed.
Our hearts sank. We decided that she should try another
dealership and get several quotes before we moved forward. But as she walked away from the dealership, the
sales manager chased her down and said, "Wait! My boss
just told me he wants to buy that car for his wife." The
new offer was $800 more than what we currently owed
and almost $7,000 more than the price they had given
us only fifteen minutes before! We couldn't believe it.
God moved in this situation, and I fully believe it was
simply because we stepped out in the faith that only
comes from God.

Now, I am not claiming that when you take a step like this the
same thing will happen to you. (For the record, when my wife
and I downsized and sold our house, the guy buying it didn't offer
us a similar deal.) But what's important is that whether we take
such steps in our families, small groups, small churches, or large
churches, we will find great joy in gospel-driven giving to the glory
of God.

And notice the theme in all these stories. In each case it was
not an issue of giving up or letting go of bad things. The church
programs, the new car, and even my son's Goldfish snack were
good things. But they were good things that were preventing far
better things from happening.

WHERE WE BEGIN

If we want to unleash the people of God in the church for the glory of God in the world, we need to let go of some good things. And we need to begin by asking ourselves some questions.

Are you and I personally willing to put everything in our lives on the table for Christ to determine what needs to stay and what needs to go?

Are your church and mine willing to put on the table every program we've created, every position we've established, every innovation we've adopted, every building we've constructed, every idea we've formulated, every team we've assembled, and every activity we've organized? Are we willing to ask God if there is a better way to use the time, energy, and money he has given us for his glory in the world?

Are you and I willing to say, "Lord, we don't want to settle for good things as your people. We want only your best"?

When we take this step of surrender and obedience together, we will find ourselves becoming part of a movement of God's people who are accomplishing God's purpose.

CHAPTER TWO

THE GOSPEL
MISUNDERSTOOD

If we want to see the people of God unleashed in the church, we need to start with the gospel of God in Christians. After all, putting everything in our lives on the table before God is the natural overflow of the gospel. Yet confusion abounds concerning the gospel in the church today.

Imagine a man I'll call Andy. A few years ago Andy professed his faith in Christ. Since that day, Andy has always espoused salvation by grace alone through faith alone. According to Andy, his actions have nothing to do with his salvation, and unfortunately this is evident in his life. Sure, he goes to church and attends his small group, but Christ is not clear in his character or his care for others. Andy turns a blind eye to the lost, even those who have never heard of Christ, and he turns a deaf ear to the cries of the poor, even those who are among his family in Christ. Though he boldly claims belief in the gospel, there is no fruit of faith in his life beyond the religious routine of cultural Christianity.

Or imagine Ashley. All her life she has been in the church. In fact, she's been baptized four times. She has listened to sermon after sermon and been in study after study where she has learned what she needs to do for God. She wants to please God, and she works hard at putting Christianity into action. Yet she never feels as if she has done enough, and she is never sure of her salvation. Trying to live out the gospel is wearing Ashley out.

Both Andy and Ashley attend Brook Hills, and I'm guessing they attend your church as well. Andy thinks work has nothing to do with salvation, and Ashley thinks work has everything to do with salvation. Both are confused. Both are wrong. And until they get a right understanding of the gospel, they will never be a part of accomplishing the purpose of God.

Unleashing radical people into the world requires the gospel as our foundation and our motivation. That's why you and I must embrace a gospel that both saves us from work and saves us to work.

SAVED FROM WORK

I get frightened when I think about *Radical* in Ashley's hands. Though in writing that book I tried to show the entirely unde-served grace of God toward us in the gospel, I know Ashley is prone to think, *I need to do more for God. I need to sell this posses-sion and make this pledge in order to be right before God.* Guilt will motivate her obedience, and action will be her obligation.

If you are Ashley and you read *Radical*, I must tell you something: you will never be radical enough. No matter what you do—even if you sell all your possessions and move to the most dangerous country in the world for the sake of ministry—you cannot do enough to be accepted before God. And the beauty of the gospel is that you don't have to. God so loved you that, despite your hopeless state of sin, he sent his Son—God in the flesh—to live the life you could not live. Jesus alone has kept the commands of God. He alone has been faithful enough, generous enough, and compassionate enough. Indeed, he alone has been radical enough.

Though Jesus was free from sin throughout his life, he bore the penalty of sin in his death. He took your place and your punishment, dying the death you deserved. Then he rose from the grave in victory over sin. And, Ashley, when you turn from yourself and trust in your Savior, he will cleanse you from all your rebellion and clothe you in his righteousness. The starting point of your radical life is your radical death—death to yourself and death to your every attempt to do enough before God.

The gospel has saved you from your work, and you are free from any effort to overcome your guilt before God. You can stop working and start believing. If you have never trusted in Christ like this, then I urge you to put down this book and place your faith in him. You don't have to repeat a prayer, sign a card, or sell a thing. Based on nothing you have done and everything Jesus has done—by grace alone through faith alone—God will declare you right before him.

A large part of me wants to put a period on this discussion and close the chapter right here. In fact, many people probably think

I should. "Yes, that is all," they might declare. "Don't say anything else."

But the gospel says something else.

SAVED TO WORK

All through the Bible we encounter an important truth, namely that the gospel that saves us *from* work also saves us *to* work. Right after Paul identifies salvation by grace alone through faith alone, he says that we are "created in Christ Jesus to do good works." Right after James talks about belief "in our glorious Lord Jesus Christ," he says that faith without deeds is useless and dead. In John's letter detailing the assurances we have in our salvation through faith in Christ, he describes how anyone who sees his brother in need but has no pity on him does not have the love of God in him.[1]

Now, it's important to recognize what these passages (and others like them) mean by such terms as *works, deeds,* and *acts of love.* In fact, I was reminded recently of the importance of clarifying the meaning of words.

I was in Germany, and a new friend there asked me, "Do you want to join some of us guys for a pickup game of football?"

"Count me in," I told him.

To my surprise, when I got down to the field, I did not find tall goalposts and a brown ball with pointy ends. Instead, I saw two goals with nets on them and a round black-and-white ball. That's when I remembered: football in Europe (and most of the rest of the world) is a lot different from my understanding of football. I call their kind of football *soccer*.

Football. Same term, two meanings.

So when I say—and when the Bible teaches—that the gospel saves us *to* work, I need to clarify what is meant by *work*.

Often Scripture refers to work in a negative sense, as actions fueled by the flesh that do not honor God. This is the way Paul frequently talks about works, and it's why he constantly condemns works as a means of salvation.[2] We are not saved by our works or through our works, for nothing we do can merit righteousness before God.[3] As mentioned earlier, the gospel saves us *from* this kind of work.

But there are also times when Scripture refers to work in a positive sense, as actions fueled by faith that bring great glory to God. Every time James refers to works or deeds or actions, he is talking about them positively. He is talking about love for the needy, mercy for the poor, and care for the suffering that flow from faith in Christ. Paul does the same thing when he talks about "work produced by faith," "every act prompted by your faith," and faith expressing itself through acts of love.[4]

So, if you are Andy, I want to tell you something important: so-called faith without acts prompted by that faith is a farce. Real faith always creates fruit.

Scripture is full of examples of faith producing work. Abraham's belief in God led him to offer his son as a sacrifice before God. Rahab's belief in God led her to risk her life for God. Paul "worked harder" than others because he believed in the grace of

God. He labored and struggled for God out of the overflow of faith in Christ.[5]

The reality is that when you believe in Christ for salvation, you not only are declared right before God as Father, but you also begin to walk with God as friend. In addition to new birth, Jesus gives you new life: a life of joyful obedience and overflowing love.[6] So when you hear Christ's radical call to live sacrificially, you do not think, *In the gospel I am free to flout his commands.* Instead you think, *In the gospel I am free to follow his commands.* And the faith that God has graciously given to you begins to produce radical fruit from you.

True faith in Christ inevitably produces great work for Christ, not works fueled by the flesh in an attempt to earn our way to God, but works fueled by faith in a life that is abandoned to God. And all of it is by grace. The basis of our salvation—Christ—is a gracious gift from God. The means of our salvation—faith—is also a gracious gift from God. And the fruit of our salvation—work—is indeed a gracious gift from God. In this way the One who gives the grace ultimately gets the glory.[7]

The gospel saves us to work.

GUILT OR GOSPEL?

So how does the gospel unleash the church?

Because the gospel saves us from work, the gospel frees us from guilt. In Christ we have been declared not guilty before God. This is vitally important when the church is confronted with staggering realities in the world. We need to have our eyes opened to hundreds of millions of people in the world who are perishing without the gospel and starving without food or water. But if we are not careful, these statistics may only create a constant, low-grade sense of guilt for never doing enough. Guilt like this will be both an unbearable burden and an unsustainable motivator. We may change our ways for a short time based upon guilt, but true and lasting life change will happen only when we believe the gospel. For when we believe the gospel, we find ourselves constantly reminded that it is never about our doing enough. We can't do enough. We can, though, trust in Christ, who has done enough.

And as we trust in Christ, he changes our hearts, minds, and lives. He transforms how we see, feel, and act. We begin to see the startling realities of the world through the eyes of a Savior who surrendered his life for the salvation of the nations. And as we grow in relational intimacy with Christ through the gospel, we gradually overflow in radical living for Christ. Any low-grade sense of guilt gets conquered by a high-grade sense of gospel that compels a willing, urgent, joyful, uncompromising, grace-saturated, God-glorifying obedience in us. We live sacrificially, not because we feel guilty, but because we have been loved greatly and now find satisfaction in sacrificial love for others. We live radically, not because we have to, but because we want to.

GOSPEL-DRIVEN ADOPTION

Let me illustrate.

A widespread adoptive culture had infused the church I pastor before I arrived. When Heather and I came to Brook Hills, we were already in the process of adopting our first son. But we didn't know many people who had adopted, and we sometimes felt like an anomaly among our friends. So when we began to share with folks at Brook Hills that we were walking through the adoption process, we expected them to be surprised and intrigued. On the contrary, our journey seemed to be the norm at Brook Hills. We found out that families at Brook Hills adopted four or five children at a time!

This adoptive culture has only grown in recent years. Last year as we were studying the book of James (once again, be forewarned!), we were about to reach a text you may know well: "Religion that God our Father accepts as pure and faultless is this: to look after orphans and widows in their distress and to keep oneself from being polluted by the world."[8] In preparation for the sermon on that particular text, I called the Department of Human Resources (DHR) in our county to find out if they had any needs in orphan or foster care.

When I put my question to the DHR director, she laughed. "Yes!" she exclaimed. "We have tons of needs!"

Well, I wanted to know, how many families would DHR need in order to take care of all the foster and adoption needs in our county?

More laughter.

"No, really," I said. "If a miracle were to take place, how many families would be sufficient to cover all the different needs you have?"

She collected herself for a minute. Then she gave me her answer. "It would be a miracle if we had 150 more families."

Can you tell where this story is going?

The day came when I preached from James 1:27. At the close I gave our church an unusual invitation: "If Christ in you is compelling you to be a part of serving children in our county in this way, then please come to a meeting two weeks from today."

By then the wonderful folks at DHR had given us all kinds of moving photographs and videos of needy children. But we wanted to be careful not to motivate God's people through emotional manipulation. So we didn't use any of it.

When the meeting time came, people from our faith family poured into our auditorium. Before the meeting began, one of the DHR workers pulled me aside and with tears in her eyes said, "What made you decide to do this? And how did you get all these people to participate?"

I smiled. "I didn't decide to do this," I said. "God decided this was important for his people. And he is the one who is compelling us to participate."

That night more than 160 families signed up to help with foster care and adoption in our county. With the gospel as our foundation and motivation, our faith family said, "We want to do all we can to make sure that every child in our county has loving arms around him or her at night. We want to point every one of these children to the Father of the fatherless and the defender of the weak, who cares for them."

As a result, our faith family is now filled with children from all over our city as well as from countries all around the world. The immense joy of foster and adoptive care has invaded our church, and our families will never be the same.

SACRIFICIAL LOVE

Yet I want to be clear about how the gospel is unleashing these families to care sacrificially for children in need. To be honest, children in the adoption and foster care systems can come with significant challenges. Some suffer from fetal alcohol syndrome and cannot sit still without acting out uncontrollably. Others have moms who were addicted to crack cocaine, and as a result their brains have been damaged in a way that will affect their behavior for the rest of their lives. Some adoptive families have new family members who are a physical threat to other children in the home.

Meet John and Karen. After having their first son, Jacob, they decided to adopt their second son, Michael, from overseas. As soon as the adoption was complete, Karen became pregnant and gave birth to a third son, Daniel, who has Down syndrome. In addition to the daily challenges of Down's, Daniel suffers from constant seizures and requires growth hormone injections. "Six days a week," John says, "I have to pin him down on the ground while Karen gives him the shot. It looks as though we will have to continue doing this until his sixteenth birthday."

Meanwhile, their adopted son, Michael, has severe learning and behavioral disabilities that require constant attention and individual supervision. He has already been removed from more than one preschool. John told me that these years are challenging his marriage, his family, and his relationship with God in ways he and Karen never could have imagined.

John and Karen are not alone. They are joined by parents who are struggling to love children whose defense mechanisms resist that love at every turn. Some children cocoon themselves in isolation, while others lash out in aggression. Many children have been physically or sexually abused, and in some situations these children become abusive themselves. My aim is not to present a harsh picture of adoption, and certainly not all stories look like these, but I want to be clear about the realities of some children in need.

So what is going to sustain John, Karen, and a host of other parents in the midst of such circumstances? What is going to motivate them to keep going when they are at the end of themselves and don't know what to do? Surely a low-grade sense of guilt would be gone by now. And any dream of having a cute family picture to send out with a Christmas card during the holiday season has been forgotten. The only thing that will sustain and strengthen these families to press on is a gospel that saves them from work and saves them to work.

John and Karen know they cannot do this on their own. They cannot provide and care for the needs of their family through their own resources alone. John recently e-mailed me and said, "Pastor, please pray that I will embrace with joy all the challenges and difficulties that come with being a father to these two. God has ordained it, and God is good."

For parents like John and Karen, God-dependent faith is the only foundation for God-glorifying work.

Still, some might hear stories like this and think, *Well, obviously these families never should have adopted.* Or, *If they were responsible people, they would have never gotten into these situations.* But these parents see it differently. What strikes me most often in my interactions with them isn't their struggles but their joy.

In a recent journal entry, Karen wrote about the delight she experienced when she and John celebrated Michael's latest birthday:

> We all went into his room this morning to tell him,
> "Happy birthday!" While I was dressing him, he was
> jumping up and down with the biggest smile. Then he
> said, "Thank you for giving me a birthday."
>
> I was quiet for a moment. I felt those words were
> not just from him but a gift from God.
>
> He wouldn't have had a "birthday" in the orphanage.
> He wouldn't have had a T-shirt with his name on it or a
> family to make him a cake and sing to him. It's not that
> these things in and of themselves are important, but they
> are the little things a family does for you and with you,
> things I take for granted. Having people there no matter
> what, having someone come when you cry, being able to
> make bad choices and still be loved.
>
> Michael is a tough kid, and none of us will ever know
> what he experienced his first two years of life, but I know
> God has created him exactly how he wants him to be.
> Although there are many days when he can make me
> want to pull my hair out, I am so grateful that God made
> me his mommy.

Indeed, gospel-driven obedience produces gospel-filled joy.

The gospel is the key to—and the only sustainable motivation for—sacrificial living. The gospel reminds us that each of us was once a child of wrath, filled with evil desires and unable to control our sinfulness. Yet God sought us and saved us. In love he adopted us as his sons and daughters. And now when we see a child who is left alone or hard to love, we can gladly bring that child into our family. Why? Because we believe the gospel. For us that means sacrificial love is not just our duty but our delight.

THE GOSPEL IS THE REASON

The gospel is the reason for radical living. The gospel is the reason a family I talked with last week is moving with their infant child to live among one of the most dangerous unreached people groups in the world. The gospel is the reason a family sold their large house in the suburbs to move into a small home in a low-income inner-city community. The gospel is the reason business leaders are leveraging their assets to aid impoverished churches. The gospel is the reason college seniors are turning their backs on the American dream and senior adults are backing out of the American dream in order to pursue a higher goal. The gospel is the reason Christians are changing their routines, adjusting their budgets, adding to their families, augmenting their plans, altering their ideas, and sacrificing their lives to accomplish the global purpose of God. Indeed, when the gospel of God is clear in the church, Christians will work hard by the grace of God with great delight for the glory of God.

We must avoid becoming churches full of Ashleys who are continually working hard to earn the approval of God while ultimately wearing out in our assignment from God. Pastors and others in leadership must be particularly careful here. I am humbled when I consider some of my own choices and how I have at times pushed the people of God to work without shepherding them with grace. Yes, the gospel saves us to work, but we must be careful to plant every challenge, every declaration, every decision, every action, every question, every confession, and every exhortation solidly in the soil of gospel grace. Only people who are resting constantly in the righteousness of Christ will be able to risk it all wholeheartedly for the glory of Christ.

And we must also avoid becoming churches full of Andys who are constantly defending the gospel while rarely demonstrating it. Again, for pastors and other leaders, the caution here is clear. The people you and I lead in the church will never be what they cannot see. Therefore, it is our call not only to preach a gospel of radical grace but also to portray a life of radical goodness. Those who espouse sound doctrine in the church should embody selfless devotion in the world. Whatever our roles in our local body, you and I are fooling ourselves if our lives lack love for the lost or compassion for the poor.

Together, let us believe God as we beg him to produce the fruit of the gospel among us. Let's show in the church a gospel that saves us from work and saves us to work.

CHAPTER THREE

GOD IS SAYING
SOMETHING

THE WORD DOES THE WORK.

Some years ago I sat near the front in a worship service and watched the guest preacher pace back and forth across the stage. He was a popular speaker in our area, and crowds had come to hear what he had to say. My first clue that something wasn't right was when he started by saying, "I forgot my Bible tonight."

But that didn't deter him. He explained that for days he had prayed about what God wanted him to say to us. He told stories about how he had taken walks in his neighborhood, sat at coffee shops, and reclined in his study. He was funny, witty, and engaging, and he kept the crowd entertained.

When he came to his conclusion, these were his exact words: "I tried to do everything I could to figure out what God wanted to say to us, but nothing ever came to my mind. So maybe that means God simply doesn't have anything to say to us tonight." With that, he prayed and walked off the stage.

I sat there with my Bible in my hands, dumbfounded. *God doesn't have anything to say to us tonight?* There I was, holding a library of sixty-six books that are decidedly and definitively the Word of God, and this guy had just said that God doesn't have a word for us? In my mind I said to this guy, "Just open this book anywhere—to Leviticus, for all I care—and read it, and you've got a word from God. Save yourself the walk around the neighborhood and the cost of your mocha. Just read the book, and God is saying something to us."

I am thankful for that experience, for it burned a permanent brand into my heart and mind. In our lives and in the church, we are never without revelation from God. At all times you and I have his message to us in all its power, authority, clarity, and might. We don't have to work to come up with a word from God; we simply have to trust the Word he has already given us. When we do, the Word of God will accomplish the work of God among the people of God.

DEPENDENT ON THE WORD

For a moment I want to speak specifically to pastors, staff members, small-group leaders, and other influencers among God's people. Practically, how do we motivate and mobilize individuals in the church to abandon their lives for the glory of God in the world?

According to countless books and conferences, you and I need to be innovative and creative. We need an entrepreneurial spirit combined with an engaging persona. Strangely, though, none of these characteristics are mentioned in the Bible as qualifications for leadership in the church. Instead, Jesus tells all his followers that, in order to make disciples, they must be able to teach people to obey God's Word. Scripture is clear that any leader who wants to unleash the people of God in the church for the glory of God in the world must simply be competent to communicate and faithful to follow the Word of God.[1]

This truth brings comfort and confidence to me as a leader in the church.

I remember when the Church at Brook Hills began talking with me about becoming their pastor. Heather and I had temporarily relocated to Atlanta after Hurricane Katrina. We were waiting to figure out how we would get back to New Orleans, where I had been teaching in a seminary. During that same time the pastor at Brook Hills resigned, and the church began the search for a replacement. A few months later I preached at Brook Hills simply to fill in. Before I knew it, I had become the interim pastor. I told them I would be glad to preach on Sundays whenever I was available over the next few months but that Heather and I would be moving back to New Orleans as soon as possible.

One Sunday morning after I had preached at Brook Hills, I got in the car to make the three-hour drive back to Atlanta. As I crossed the border between Alabama and Georgia, I received a call. The chairman of the pastor search team was on the other end. He said, "David, would you be able to meet with us next week about you potentially becoming our next pastor?"

What?

I had never even thought about pastoring. I loved teaching at the seminary and traveling around the world with students, sharing the gospel. I had no desire to do anything different.

Besides, what were they thinking? Clearly I was not the best person for this church. For starters, I had never been a pastor. The last thing such a large church needed was a rookie. What's more, I had no clue how to be a part of, much less to lead, such a large church. The church of which I was a member in New Orleans had two hundred people on a high-attendance Sunday. Brook Hills had thousands of members and a multimillion-dollar budget. I didn't even know how to handle my family's meager finances.

Still, I wanted to be considerate. I was honored by their invitation, so I told the chairman, "Heather and I would be glad to have lunch with you all next week, but I am certain the Lord is not leading me to be your next pastor."

Famous last words.

Heather and I met with the team the following week. I came armed with reasons why they would not want me to be their pastor. With airtight logic I explained how obvious it was that they needed someone with pastoral experience, professional capability, and personal wisdom—all of which I lacked. After I had made my case for why this conversation needn't go any further, Heather and I got in our car, all the more determined to go back to New Orleans.

But the Lord had different plans. Over the coming weeks God coordinated a variety of circumstances to bring the search team—and us—to the conclusion that the Lord was indeed leading me to pastor this church. But the question still persisted at the forefront of my mind: *How do I pastor this church?* What I did *not* bring to the task simply overwhelmed me.

And that's when God reminded me of what I did bring: his Word. "Apart from me," Jesus says, "you can do nothing.… If you remain in me and my words remain in you,…you [will] bear much fruit."[2] God reminded me that my ability to lead his people was ultimately not dependent on my experience or my ingenuity. My ability to lead his people was (and is) dependent on his power that is alive in his Spirit and at work in his truth.

During that time I was also reading David Brainerd's diary. Brainerd, as you may know, was a faithful missionary who spent years preaching the Scriptures among Native Americans. Brainerd would often write in his journal about how utterly incapable he was of accomplishing the work to which God had called him. He was constantly overwhelmed by his own inadequacy. Based upon Brainerd's example, I began to pray, "Lord, let me make a difference for you that is utterly disproportionate to who I am."[3] Thanks to Brainerd, this has been my continual prayer, not just in the pastor search process that led me to the Church at Brook Hills, but also in the day-to-day process now of leading the Church at Brook Hills.

The reality is that I'm still a beginner as a pastor, in over my head at every level. I often feel like Solomon when he said, "I am only a little child and do not know how to carry out my duties."[4] I need wisdom—the kind of wisdom that comes only from the Bible.

God has designed us to depend on his Word to lead his people in ways that are utterly disproportionate to who we are.

THE WORD IN ACTION

The only wise basis for an act of radical obedience is God him-self—the author, creator, and ruler of our lives—commanding such action. Christians would be foolish to make radical sacrifices or to take radical risks in their lives simply because someone in the church suggested it. That's why dependence on God's Word is his design for all of us, not just the leaders. As members of churches, we stake our lives—and his church—on truth from God, not thoughts from men and women. For this reason, mem-bers of churches should desire and, in a sense, demand nothing less than continual feasts on God's Word in the church. This alone will satisfy, strengthen, and spread the church in the world.

When I began pastoring at Brook Hills, I spent many Sundays describing the supremacy of the Bible and explaining how it must be central in all our plans, priorities, and programs. I tried to make clear that, apart from God's Word, I was helpless as a leader and we were powerless as a church. But attuned to God's Word, together we could be a part of accomplishing God's purpose in the world.

Without a doubt everything God has done and is doing among our faith family has been built upon the foundation of our studying God's Word. You've already seen what happened when we grappled honestly with the book of James. I could name many other examples. When we came to Matthew 7:13–27, we were frightened by the portrait of men and women who deceive them-selves into thinking they are right before God when they are not. That led us to foundational texts such as Romans 3, John 3,

Philippians 1–2, and 1 John, which show what the gospel is, how the gospel saves us, how the gospel works in us, and how the gospel guarantees the completion of our salvation.

The more we studied the gospel in God's Word, seeing how the gospel infiltrates every facet of our lives, the more I found myself asking, *Do I really believe this gospel? I preach it, but do I really believe it? For if this gospel is true, then the implications for me, my church, and the world around me are staggering.* As I wrestled with these questions, personal conviction led me on a pastoral journey in which I walked our church through biblical truths that I hope are accurately expressed in *Radical.*

As we explored those truths, I began sensing a tendency in our people to define holiness by how much we do for God. Amid all our talk of radical obedience, we were losing sight of gospel grace. This concern led me next to preach through Galatians, where God reminds us of the centrality of grace in the life of faith. Not long after studying Galatians is when we walked through James, and God showed us how his grace in our faith works to his glory. Taken together, these immersions in Bible books compelled us to take risks that we had never taken before and to make decisions that we had never made before.

In short, the Word of God accomplishes the work of God. Some of my favorite moments in the church are when people come to me and say, "Pastor, I think you're crazy for saying some of the things you say." Then they follow up (most of the time!) with these words: "But you're only saying what God has said, so I guess we need to obey." When the words of mere humans drive how and where we are going, we will get nowhere. When we

unchain the power of God's Word in the church, it will unleash
the potential of God's people in the world.

THE PROBLEM WITH HELPING GOD

Please note that I am not espousing a certain methodology for
teaching and preaching the Bible, whether that be topical, narrative, verse by verse, verse with verse, dialogical, or doctrinal. My
intent is simply to say that if we want to make God's glory known
in the world, then we must make the teaching of God's Word central in the church.[5] We are fooling ourselves if we think we can
advance the church any other way.

But you might be wondering, is that all? That's how to
unleash a radical people for the glory of God in the world—just
teach God's Word in the church? How radical is that? And isn't
everyone already doing it?

Unfortunately, everyone is not already doing it. Many voices
today, in fact, are claiming that teaching or preaching the Bible
simply doesn't work as well as it used to. For instance, not long ago
I listened to a lecture from a "church innovator" who boldly proclaimed that the spoken word no longer communicates as it once
did. He said, "If you want to get your point across to people today,
you must make your point musically."

I'm suspicious. After thousands of years of effective communication through the spoken word, I don't think we've quite
reached the zenith in history that this man surmised. (In addition, I found it ironic that he chose to speak, not sing, his lecture.)

Even among those who stand by the spoken word, many lack confidence in the sufficiency of God's Word. They sometimes point out that the Bible doesn't speak directly to the situations that people are experiencing today. In every church, parents struggle with rebellious kids, single moms enter divorce recovery, men and women find themselves in financial straits, businesspeople face daunting challenges at work, and families suffer through the cancer of a loved one. Do we really think (these objectors might say) that teaching about the Israelites and the Moabites will help our members in need?

As a result of this lack of confidence, churches may begin to minimize God's Word. It's not necessarily that we think Bible teaching is unimportant. We just don't believe it's enough. Members of the church want something else, and so those of us who lead the church give something else. In our small groups and from the pulpit, we read a verse or two, maybe a story, and then we supplement it with our own motivational thoughts, moving stories, creative ideas, and personal opinions. We glean help from the latest Christian books, the most promising leadership fads, the newest recovery advice, the sharpest financial counsel, and the best opinions on marriage and family. Our motives, of course, are admirable. We want to serve people in need far better than a sermon on the Israelites and Moabites could. Still, in the words of Walter Kaiser, "Pastors have decided that using the Bible is a handicap for meeting the needs of the [different] generations; therefore they have gone to drawing their sermons from the plethora of recovery and pop-psychology books that fill our Christian bookstores. The market-forces demand that we give them what they want to hear if we wish them to return and pay for the mega-sanctuaries that we have built."[6]

Do you see the problem that can result from our good intentions? We can soon find ourselves scaling the heights of arrogance. For at this point we are assuming that God has not given us enough in his Word, and we are acting as if he needs us to supplement his communication to his people with our own talks and thoughts every week.

But God is not in heaven thinking, *Man, if only I would have known or thought about this struggle or that situation my people would walk through in the twenty-first century, I would have addressed it. I am so thankful for wise leaders who are helping me in areas I left out!* Obviously this is not the case. God has given us everything we need in the Word we have.

"But what we have does not address so many situations in people's lives today," some might say. And this is true. But God's design in his Word is not to provide all the practical guidelines, parenting tips, leadership advice, and financial counsel that Americans are looking for in the twenty-first century. Instead, the purpose of God's Word is to transform people in every country and every century into the image of Jesus. The Bible is sufficient to accomplish this task, and God knows this is what people need most.

No leader in the church can be expected to give people all the answers they want or need on parenting, marriage, money management, and every other issue in life. No leader is that good, and God has designed it this way so that the church never fosters an unhealthy dependence on, or an unhealthy admiration of, any particular leader in the church.

The Bible is not in a church leader's hands so he or she can give people answers to every question they have and guidance for every situation they face. Instead, the Bible is in a church leader's hands to transform people into the image of Christ and to get people in touch with the Holy Spirit of God, who will not only give them counsel for every situation they face but will also walk with them through those situations. And when church leaders use God's Word for this purpose, then church members develop a healthy dependence on God's Spirit and a healthy admiration of God's glory.

When you think about it this way, the Israelites and Moabites are definitely worth talking about. For example, it's worth looking at how Lot's incestuous relationship with his daughter created the despised Moabites. It's worth reading how Israelite men were later seduced by Moabite women into sexual immorality, with thousands of Israelite men dying as a result. It's worth seeing all of that to know that one day, in the most unexpected way, God pursued an undeserving Moabite woman named Ruth. In her otherwise hopeless situation, God turned her suffering into her satisfaction. He grafted her into an Israelite family where her line would one day lead to the birth of Jesus, the Savior of the world.[7]

How is this going to help people walk through twenty-first century struggles? It will remind all the businesspeople in the church that they needn't worry about spending their lives climbing a ladder when the God of the universe has pursued them by his grace, not based on what they have done, but based on who he is. It will remind the family dealing with cancer that God is indeed sovereign and that in their suffering he may actually be plotting their satisfaction. It will remind all the people of God that the highest privilege of our lives is not found in who we know, where we live, what we achieve, or how much money we make. Our highest privilege is found in being a part of the family line of Jesus, in whom we have life and for whom we live.

The Word does this work.

The question is, will we let it? As leaders and influencers in the church, will we turn aside from our wit, our thoughts, our counsel, and our advice to give people God's Word instead? As members in the church, will we trust that God knew what he was doing when he gave us his Word? Together, will we realize that our greatest need is not to be successful business executives, profitable money managers, or even good parents but to know God and to walk with him?

Now we're getting to the heart of how God moves his people.

THE PLAN HE HAS ALREADY
PROMISED TO BLESS

Let's take this line of reasoning one step further. God's Word is clearly the foundation for teaching and preaching in the church, but what if his revelation is also the foundation for strategizing and planning in the church? What if the Bible is intended not only to dictate our theology but also to determine our methodology?

Just as I am tempted to interject my thoughts and opinions into preaching in the church, so I also find myself tempted to interpose my ideas into planning for the church. I love to dream about what we can accomplish for the kingdom of God and then to diagram the steps we need to take to achieve it all. I love to sit around with other members of the church who want to glorify God and who have been given creative gifts from God and together to craft plans and strategies for the church. I can walk away from such conversations with great anticipation in my mind and great zeal in my heart for God to bless our work for his name's sake.

But there is a subtly deceptive, ultimately dangerous assumption inherent in doing things this way. The assumption is that God is somehow obligated to bless the plans we create. Yet nowhere in Scripture has God promised to bless my plans or anyone else's in the church, no matter how innovative or creative they may be. Neither has God promised to bless us based solely on our motives. Sure, we are supposed to do everything for the glory of God, but that doesn't mean everything we do for his glory is assured of his blessing.[8]

There is only one thing God has promised to bless, and that is his plan.[9] He has given us his plan in his Word, and if we want the blessing of God, then we don't need to come up with something else. Instead, we need to align with the plan he has already promised to bless.

When I came to Brook Hills, multiple phases of a building project remained to be finished. The plan was to expand the lobby into a more spacious and inviting environment for guests, to build additional classrooms, and to begin construction on sports fields adjacent to our parking lot. The plan seemed good, and people were excited about it. The creative energies of church leaders, combined with the abundant resources of church members, had made this plan possible, and people were ready to get started.

Then we began asking, "Does this plan best align with the plan of God?"

As we took this question to Scripture, we saw a clear plan from the mouth of Jesus: Make disciples of all the nations. Take up your cross, follow me, and lead others to follow me in the same way. Jesus never told us to build lobby space, create more classrooms, or design sports fields. Not that it would necessarily be wrong to do these things. After all, Jesus never commanded us to build bathrooms either, but we have those. When it came to our plans then, the question was, Is this the best (notice: not *good* but *best*) way to align with the plan Jesus *has* laid before us?

Is building a nicer, more comfortable lobby the best way to use our resources to lead people to take up a cross and follow Christ? Is building more space for classes the best way to help people obey Christ? Is building soccer fields in Birmingham the best strategy for spreading the gospel to the ends of the earth (particularly when so many have never even heard the gospel)?

They might be. But you and I have to ask.

And as we asked these questions at Brook Hills, our decision became clear. Instead of expanding the lobby for our church, we would use that money to start planting other churches. Instead of constructing more classrooms where we could listen to more lectures, we would become more intentional about gathering in our homes, where we could better share our lives. And instead of building more soccer fields in our community, we would use that money to serve spiritually and physically impoverished peoples around the world. (Interestingly, we have members in our faith family now using sports fields in slums around the world to serve and start churches.)

In our decision we believed we were exchanging good, well-intentioned plans that we had hoped God would bless for better, Word-driven plans that God had guaranteed to bless.

Now, I want to clarify what I mean (and don't mean) by the blessing of God. I am not saying that if the Word is primary in our churches, then we will be popular in the world. In many ways we can expect the opposite to be true. If crowds of people hated the words of Jesus in the first century, we can certainly expect them to feel the same way in the twenty-first century.[10] The blessing of God does not mean acceptance by the world.

Similarly, I am not implying that teaching and studying God's Word in the church bring instant results. The process of sanctification in Christians and mobilization in the church takes time and requires patience. The challenge for church members and leaders alike is to faithfully hold fast to God's Word, trusting that ultimately God will use it to accomplish his intended, eternal, global purpose.[11]

A WORD WE CAN TRUST

I wish you could have slipped into the auditorium at Brook Hills around midnight last Friday evening. Every seat was taken, and some sat in the aisles. Everyone had their Bibles open, and almost everyone was still taking notes, soaking in the Word of God as it was being taught. We call it Secret Church—an event patterned after underground house churches around the world who gather for hours at a time to study Scripture. In Birmingham last Friday, from 6:00 p.m. straight until almost 1:00 a.m., several thousand men and women simply studied the Word and prayed together. College students from faraway campuses sat next to eighty-year-olds from various churches. As these believers listened attentively and engaged passionately, I was reminded again that we don't have to engineer something entertaining to win an audience. The Word is sufficient to hold the attention of God's people and satisfying enough to capture their affection.

You and I can trust this Word. It forms and fulfills, motivates and mobilizes, equips and empowers, leads and directs the people of God in the church for the plan of God in the world. This won't automatically make everything easy in the church. But as long as Christians together are prayerfully and humbly asking what the plan of God is in his Word for his people and are abandoning our lives to it, we will be unleashing a radical people.

And what, then, *is* God's plan? That question sets the stage for what may be a surprising answer.

CHAPTER FOUR

THE GENIUS
OF WRONG

BUILDING THE RIGHT CHURCH DEPENDS ON USING ALL THE WRONG PEOPLE.

I was sitting at a table with an old friend who leads a large and thriving church. "We try to make everything easy for the members of our church," he said to me. "We encourage them to get to know people in our community, whether in their neighborhood or office or anywhere else. Then all they have to do is invite those people to church. At church, those people will hear relevant, gifted communicators in a warm, attractive, and appealing environment where their children can be a part of top-of-the-line programs."

He concluded, "If our members will just invite their friends to the environment we create, then we can take care of the rest."

Then he asked me what we do at Brook Hills.

Hesitantly I said, "We actually do the exact opposite."

"Oh really," he said. "What do you mean?"

"Well, when we gather as the church, our main focus is on the church. In other words, we organize our worship environment around believers, not unbelievers."

He looked confused. "Why would you do that?" he asked. "If your worship environment on Sunday is not appealing to non-Christians, then how is your church going to intentionally lead unbelievers in Birmingham to Christ?"

"We're going to equip our people every Sunday to lead unbelievers in Birmingham to Christ all week long," I said.

"Your members are going to lead them to Christ?"

"That's our plan."

"Well," he said, "once those unbelievers become believers, how are they going to grow in Christ?"

"Our people are going to be equipped to show new believers how to live as followers of Christ," I said. "I want people in the church to be able to fulfill the purpose for which they were created without being dependent on gifted preachers, nice buildings, and great programs to do it for them."

Looking puzzled, he said, "Well, that's a new approach."

Now, again, I am a young pastor, and I have a lot to learn, particularly from pastors like this one, whom I respect greatly. But I don't think I'm coming up with something new here.

I believe in the people of God. Or more specifically, I believe in the work of God's Spirit through God's Word in God's people. The last thing I want to do is rob Christians of the joy of making disciples by telling them that I or anyone or anything else can take care of that for them.

Someone might ask, "But if a church has a gifted communicator or a gifted leader, wouldn't we want as many people as possible to hear that person?"

The answer is "not necessarily." The goal of the church is never for one person to be equipped and empowered to lead as many people as possible to Christ. The goal is always for all of God's people to be equipped and empowered to lead as many people as possible to Christ.

I also believe in the plan of God. In Jesus' simple command to "make disciples," he has invited every one of his followers to share the life of Christ with others in a sacrificial, intentional, global effort to multiply the gospel of Christ through others. He never intended to limit this invitation to the most effective communicators, the most brilliant organizers, or the most talented leaders and artists—all the allegedly right people that you and I are prone to exalt in the church. Instead, the Spirit of God has empowered every follower of Christ to accomplish the purpose of God for the glory of God in the world. This includes the so-called wrong people: those who are the least effective, least brilliant, or least talented in the church.

Building the right church, then, is dependent on using all the wrong people.

MANUFACTURED ELEMENTS

At one point in *Radical*, I described the various elements that we in America have manufactured for growing a church.[1] I want to revisit the discussion I began there and take it further so we can better explore what a church might look like if it properly valued the wrong people.

It's commonly assumed that if you and I want to be a part of a growing church today, we need a few simple elements.

First, we need a good performance. In an entertainment-driven culture, we need someone who can captivate the crowds. If we don't have a charismatic communicator, we're sunk from the start. Even if we have to show him on video, we get a good speaker. And for a bonus, we surround the speaker with quality music and arts.

Next, we need a place to hold the crowds who will come. This usually means investing hundreds of thousands, if not millions, of dollars in a facility to house the performance. The more attractive the environment, the better.

Then once the crowds get there, we need something to keep them coming back. So we start programs—first-class, top-of-the-line programs—for kids, youth, and families, for every age and stage. And in order to have those programs, we need professionals to run them. That way parents can drop their kids off at the door, and the professionals can handle ministry for them. We don't want people trying this at home.

There it is: a performance at a place filled with programs run by professionals. The problem, though, is the one *p* we have left out of the equation: the people of God.

PEOPLE, NOT PERFORMANCES

What if growing the church was never intended to depend on creating a good performance with all the right people on the stage?

Where did we get the idea that this was necessary? Certainly Scripture instructs us to gather for worship.[2] This is nonnegotiable but not necessarily in the way we usually think about it.

Imagine being in a church on the other side of the world where it is illegal for the church even to exist. You wait until midnight, when everyone else in the village is asleep, to quietly leave your house. Under the cover of darkness, you sneak down winding roads and past silent houses, looking around every corner to make sure no one is following you. You know that if you or anyone else from your church is caught, you may never see your home again. For that matter, you may never see the light of day again.

Yet you continue on until you round a bend, and there you see a small house with a faint light emanating from it. Checking one last time to make sure you have not been tailed, you slip inside. There you are greeted by a small band of brothers and sisters who have made the same long trek. As you look at their weary but expectant faces, you realize something: Not one of them has come because a great communicator has been scheduled to speak. Not one is present because a cool band is scheduled to play. No, all are there simply because they desire to gather with the people of God, and they are willing to risk their lives to be together.

Performance has nothing to do with it. People have everything to do with it.

Whenever I am in churches overseas like the one just depicted, I am reminded of how much we have filled our contemporary worship environments with performance elements such as elaborate stage sets, state-of-the-art sound systems, and high-definition video screens. I am also struck by our reliance upon having just the right speaker and just the right musician who can attract the most people to a worship service. But what if the church itself—the people of God gathered in one place—is intended to be the attraction, regardless of who is teaching or singing that day? This is enough for our brothers and sisters around the world.

But is it enough for us?

I am haunted by this question on Sundays as I stand in a nice auditorium with a quality sound system and large video screens on the wall, all designed to spotlight select people on stage. It's not that everything in this scene is necessarily wrong, but I do wonder what in this scene is biblically best and practically healthy for the people of God. I have more questions than I have answers on this issue, and I am grateful for leaders in our worship ministry who are willing to ask the questions with me.

I mentioned earlier that we recently cut 83 percent of our worship budget. We did this not only to free up resources for urgent needs around the world but also to scale back our emphasis on nonessential elements of corporate worship. We want to focus on ways we can cultivate the best people: a people who love to pray together, fast together, confess sin together, sing together, and study together; a people who depend more on the Word that is spoken than on the one who speaks it; a people who are gripped in music more by the content of the song than by the appeal of the singer; and a people who define worship less by the quality of a slick performance and more by the commitment of a humble people who gather week after week simply to behold the glory of God as they surrender their lives to him.

PEOPLE, NOT PLACES

When the church is fundamentally a gathering of committed people, the place where the church gathers hardly matters.

Over the last few years, I have had many conversations, both inside and outside Brook Hills, about church buildings. Admittedly, I pastor a church that gathers in and enjoys the luxuries of one of these multimillion-dollar edifices. Because we have this building, I want us to steward it well, whether that means maximizing it for ministry or selling it and spending our resources differently. Everything is on the table, and the Lord will lead us in what is best. I realize that a lot of people in our church have sacrificed greatly to make our facility a reality, and I am deeply grateful for God's grace in them. At the same time, I am not convinced that large buildings are the best or only way to use God's resources.

You may ask (as members of our church and leaders of other churches have asked me in countless conversations), "What's wrong with constructing church buildings? Nowhere does the New Testament say we shouldn't construct church buildings."

But that's just it. There's also nothing in the New Testament that says we *should* construct church buildings. So whenever we plant a church or whenever a church starts to grow, why is the first thing we think, *We need to spend masses of our resources on a building*? Why would we spend an inordinate amount of our resources on something that is never prescribed or even encouraged in the New Testament? Why would we not instead use those resources on that which is explicitly promoted in the New Testament, such as sharing the gospel with the lost or helping the poor in the church?[3] As I write this, more than seven hundred million people around the world live in slums. Many of them are our brothers and sisters in Christ. Should we really be prioritizing bigger buildings for ourselves?

I spoke recently with the pastor of an inner-city church plant in the southern United States. His congregation numbers around one hundred people, and recently twenty of them went on a short-term mission trip to a third-world country. As they traveled, they read and discussed *Radical* and the truths from God's Word that the book presents. By the time the team came back, God had transformed their hearts and minds in surprising ways.

They began reevaluating how they had been spending their lives and resources, both personally and corporately. When they looked at the church budget, they realized that their little church was spending five thousand dollars a month to lease building space downtown. So some of the members asked the pastor, "Why don't we take this sixty thousand dollars a year and use it for something more eternally valuable?"

"Then where are we going to meet as a church?" he asked.

They pointed to the parking deck next to the space they were leasing. "We can meet over there," they said.

"Outside?" he asked.

"It's covered, it's empty on Sundays, and we already know that it's available for our use."

The pastor gave it some thought and then said, "Let's do it." The church is now meeting outside every Sunday on a parking deck.

This is the beauty of New Testament Christianity, and I wonder if too many of us are missing it. We definitely do not have to construct buildings as houses of worship. In the words of Stephen before he was martyred by the Sanhedrin, "The Most High does not live in houses made by men."[4]

Stephen was speaking to resistant people who were undergoing a major shift in the redemptive plan of God. They were used to seeing the presence of God symbolized in the temple, a monumental edifice. But with Jesus' death on the cross, the way had been opened for people to dwell in the presence of God in any place.[5] No central building was necessary. And as a result, they no longer needed to focus on a building as a house of worship.

Well, what would the house of worship be, then?

You guessed it: people.

Paul says to the church at Corinth, "Don't you know that you yourselves are God's temple and that God's Spirit lives in you?" He later tells them that their bodies are the temple of God.[6] This is the astounding reality of New Testament religion: we as Christians are the house of worship.

So let's gather wherever we can—in homes, in offices, in workspaces, in parks, in any facilities we can find. Let's remember that many of our brothers and sisters around the world simply meet outside. And let's at least consider not spending such a large portion of our resources on building places when the priority of the New Testament is decidedly on building people.

PEOPLE, NOT PROGRAMS

The challenge, though, is that we need our places to sustain our programs. How will we have thriving children and adult programs if we don't have a place to host them? This is when we begin to realize that redefining place in ministry leads to rethinking the importance of programs in ministry.

Imagine that your church had no building or facilities whatsoever. Could you still make disciples? Certainly the answer is yes. Churches all around the world make do. So how would your church make disciples completely separate from a church building? This is the question we started asking at Brook Hills, and it has led us to some significant changes. I'll share just one.

For years we had hosted a Vacation Bible School for one week every summer in our building. Members of the church would spend hours decorating rooms and preparing facilities for the time when kids in our community would come to our building for ministry. But then our children's ministry leaders asked, "If we didn't have a building, how could we teach the gospel to kids throughout our community?"

That's when they began equipping parents, children's ministry leaders, and small-group leaders in our faith family to host Bible clubs for kids in their homes. We already had homes spread all around our immediate community. Why not make our homes the place of ministry instead of the church building? Why not invite people from our neighborhoods, not to go to a church building with us, but to come across the street and into our homes with us? Home is where we could show the gospel to their children while we also shared life with them.

So during the summer, members of our church started hosting neighbors in their homes for Bible clubs. Crowds of kids came—far more than we could ever have hosted in our church building at one time. And all of it took place in diverse neighbor-hoods far away from our building.

The outcome? Scores of non-Christian neighbors are hearing a gospel-centered witness and seeing a gospel-centered family right next door, and the gospel is multiplying throughout our com-munity.

One day I visited a home during a Bible club event. As kids played in the yard and parents visited, the host mom and dad hit me with a proposal. "We were thinking that we could invite these kids and their families to our home throughout the year. We'd be doing ministry here instead of trying to do it all at the church building on a Wednesday night. Would that be okay with you?"

Yes! That would be okay with me! I am okay when people discover that God has built into our everyday lives opportunities and platforms to spread the gospel. I am okay when people real-ize that we are not dependent on well-crafted programs at desig-nated places to accomplish the mission God has created us for as his people.

This is just one small illustration in the area of children's min-istry. But imagine what could happen if this picture were multi-plied across the church: men and women seeing that the most effective avenues for ministry are found not in programs created for them but amid the people who surround them where they live. God has given every follower of Christ natural avenues to spread the gospel and declare his glory. Which means that the last thing leaders should do is pull people away from those avenues in order to participate in our activities.

At one point at Brook Hills, we were trying to organize and

centralize all the types of ministry in which people were involved. For example, we created community ministry programs so people could participate in outreach efforts in our city. We encouraged every small group to get involved in one of the programs we had organized. The only problem was that the more Christ compelled the members of our faith family to see the opportunities he had built into their lives for the spread of the gospel, the less time they had to participate in our programs. I have to admit: when people started giving themselves to ministries we had not organized, we didn't know what to do about it.

That's when we woke up and said to ourselves, "Why are we trying to organize how and where and when our people minister? God has already given them opportunities for ministry where they live and work and play." So we decided to stop planning, creating, and managing outreach programs and to start unleashing people to maximize the ministry opportunities God had already planned and created for them.

From that point the impact of our church in the community changed radically. Now our people are busy leading Bible studies in their workplaces and neighborhoods, helping addicts in rehabilitation centers, supplying food in homeless shelters, loving orphans in learning centers, caring for widows in retirement homes, providing hospice care for the elderly, training men and women in job skills, tutoring men and women in reading, helping patients in AIDS clinics, teaching English to internationals, and serving in a variety of other ways. And now our leadership team understands that it's good when people are so involved in ministry where they live that they don't have time to participate in the programs we create.

If you are a leader in the church, think about the individuals in your care. See their faces, hear their names, and picture their lives. Consider how God has written a different story in each of their lives, filled with varied circumstances and challenges, trials and temptations, experiences and encounters. He has sovereignly led them to the life stage and situation where they now find themselves, surrounded by people you will never meet and opportunities you will never have. And you have been called by God to serve them in the accomplishment of God's purpose for their lives. If you're like me, the last thing you want to do is sideline them to sit during a performance while you do the work or to participate in a program you have created. Instead, you want to equip them, train them, support them, and set them free to use everything God has given them to make his glory known in ways you could never design or imagine.

And if you are a member of the church, start dreaming and strategizing. Consider where God has placed you, who God has put around you, and how God desires to use you for his glory where you live and work. If you are single, how can you make the most of your singleness for ministry?[7] If you are married, how can you serve together with your spouse in your community? If you have kids, how can you make your home a ministry to children in your neighborhood? If you work outside the home, how can you share Christ in your workplace? Be careful not to let programs in the church keep you from engaging people in the world with the gospel. Make the most of the opportunities for ministry that God has built into your life.

I think of Darren and Julia, a married couple in our church. Darren works in automobile service, and he intentionally uses his work as an avenue for sharing the gospel. He often tells me stories about guys he works with who have come to Christ and whom he is now personally teaching to follow Christ. Meanwhile, he and Julia serve together in a residential facility that provides shelter and rehabilitation for women. Christ is transforming numerous people's lives in our city through this one couple.

Imagine the spread of the gospel for the glory of God if every follower of Christ were involved in ministry like this. Who can fathom the potential of the church when we stop programming ministry for people and start propelling people into ministry?

PEOPLE, NOT PROFESSIONALS

That question leads to a right understanding of leaders in the church.

Unfortunately, we have a tendency to overlook God's plan for people when we organize churches around professionals. We single out people who seem especially gifted, and we craft the community of faith around them. Everything we do is dependent on their speaking ability, organizational aptitude, and creative skill. But the ministry of making disciples was not intended for professionals alone; it was intended for the whole people of God.

All men and women who have placed their faith in Christ have the Spirit in them so they might be witnesses for Christ to the

ends of the earth. When you read Acts 2, you realize that the giving of the Spirit was never to be a special anointing on a select
few. This is about a supernatural anointing on every single one of
God's people.[8]

Think about the time Jesus was talking with his disciples
about the coming of the Holy Spirit. "I tell you the truth," he
said, "anyone who has faith in me will do what I have been doing.
He will do even greater things than these, because I am going to
the Father."[9]

What did Jesus mean? Was he saying that the anointing of
the Holy Spirit on us would be stronger than it was on him? Yes.
But the key is *why* it would be stronger.

The Spirit's anointing on us is not stronger in quality than it
was on Jesus. After all, he was sinless. And as a result, his relationship with the Spirit of God was totally unhindered. So how
will the Spirit's anointing on our lives enable us to do greater
things than Jesus could do?

We will do greater things, not because of the quality of the
Spirit in select ones among us, but because of the quantity of the
Spirit spread throughout all of us. The Spirit of God does not rest
on just one individual, as we observe in Jesus. No, the Spirit of
God rests on every disciple of Jesus, and because of the filling of
the Spirit all across the community of faith, we can see greater
things than anyone ever saw in the ministry of Jesus.

At this moment, while you read this sentence, men and
women around the world are being saved from their sins through
the proclamation of the gospel. At this moment, people are being
delivered from addictions and healed of diseases. At this moment,

brothers and sisters are advancing the gospel in power amid unreached people groups. All of this is happening right now because the Spirit of God has been poured out on all his people all over the world.

Let us not, then, be so foolish as to confine the work of the Spirit to one professional, speaking in one place, at one time of the week. Let us not be so unwise as to bank the spread of the gospel on a certain person at a certain place when all week long the Spirit of God is living in every single man and woman of God, empowering each of us to advance the kingdom of God for his glory.

I was having a conversation the other day with a seminary buddy who jokingly accused me of campaigning to end paid leadership in the church, his salary (and mine) included. You might be wondering the same thing. Is there a place for paid leaders—that is, professionals—in the church?

Absolutely. And I don't think I'm saying this out of self-interest. When we look in the New Testament, we clearly see a warrant, even a command, to provide financially for certain teachers and leaders in the church. Paul says it is good for leaders who sow spiritual blessings among God's people to reap material blessings from God's people. Of course, leaders in the church must be careful to honor God by their use of money.[10]

What, then, is the responsibility of such leaders in the church? Paul answers this question in Ephesians 4. God has given leaders to the church to equip God's people for ministry and "prepare God's people for works of service."[11] The church has been entrusted by God with stewards of God's Word to equip God's people to be servants with God's Word. This goes to the essence of being radical together, and it changes everything about how we view leaders in the church.

There is clearly no way that I as a pastor can minister to all the needs in our church, much less in our city. Realizing this, some people might say, "Well, that's what the rest of the church staff is for." But that can't be true either. We will never have enough staff members to meet all the needs in our church or our city. If we want to multiply the gospel from our faith family to all the families of the earth, it will require not just a pastor or church staff but the entire body of Christ built up in love "as each part does its work."[12]

What this means, then, is that church leaders are intended by God not to plan events but to equip people. Leaders do not exist to provide services; they exist to serve people. Realizing this, we who are leaders in our faith family have made a concentrated effort to take resources (most notably our time) away from organizing ministry for people and to invest them more in mobilizing people for ministry.

As I write this, an overseas church leader I'll call Dominic comes to mind. I met him once while visiting a communist nation.

Dominic is now in his sixties, and he has been the pastor of a relatively small house church for most of his life. Dominic's passion is telling people about Christ. He was once brought before the communist council in his community to be questioned about his evangelistic work. He walked into the interrogation room with a large rock in his hands and set it down on the table in front of the men who were about to question him.

Surprised, one of the men asked Dominic, "Why did you bring this rock with you?"

Dominic replied, "Before we begin my questioning today, I want you to know something. If you try to stop me from telling people about the greatness of Jesus Christ, then this rock is going to start speaking for me." Dominic was alluding to Luke 19:40, where Jesus says that if the disciples didn't proclaim his glory, the stones would cry out instead. The communist leaders, of course, had no idea what Dominic was talking about. They conferred and decided he was out of his mind, so they released him without further questioning!

Dominic's passion to tell people about Christ translates into a commitment to train people in the church. When he leads someone to Christ, Dominic takes personal responsibility for helping that person grow in Christ. His goal is for that person to become a leader in the church and then eventually to leave and plant another church somewhere else. (Almost all church planters in that part of the world are bivocational.) Dominic's church has now planted more than sixty other churches in his country, with nearly every one of the pastors trained by Dominic. His life and leadership are a picture of what it means, not to organize ministry for people, but to mobilize people for ministry.

WHERE WILL OUR LIVES COUNT?

Isn't this the model of Jesus? During his ministry on earth, he spent more time with twelve men than with everyone else put together. In John 17, where he recounts his ministry before going to the cross, he doesn't mention the multitudes he preached to or the miracles he performed. As spectacular as those events were, they were not his primary focus. Instead, forty times Jesus speaks to and about the men in whom he had invested his life. They were his focus.

When he came to his ascension, Jesus had no buildings or programs to point to and no crowds to boast of. Indeed, most of the crowds had walked away. Just 120 unschooled, ordinary people were gathered—a small group with a small band of leaders.

And he had given them one command as their commission: make disciples. Do with others what I have done with you, Jesus had said. Don't sit in a classroom; share your lives. Don't build extravagant places; build extraordinary people. Make disciples who will make disciples who will make disciples, and together multiply this gospel to all peoples. This is the simple command that was to drive the church. And this is the simple command that is to drive each of our lives.

I don't want this command to be treated as optional in my life or in anyone else's life in the church I pastor. Personally, I have an intentional disciple-making plan that involves sharing life with and multiplying the gospel through my family, a small group of men within our church, and church planters we are sending out from our church. I don't want to imply that this plan is always smooth in practice or easy to implement. Like you, I am constantly beset by the busyness of life and the responsibilities of leadership, and if I am not careful, disciple making fades into the background. As a result, I want to act intentionally, for if I forsake the priority of people, then I will miss the purpose of God.

Every one of our pastors and church staff has designed similar disciple-making plans. In addition, we help all new members in our church to outline their plans for how they will be involved in making disciples of all nations.[13] The key for all of us is an intense desire and intentional effort to make every one of our lives count for the multiplication of the gospel in the world.

Regardless of your place in the church, remember that you are not intended to be sidelined in the kingdom of God. You may at times feel like the wrong person, thinking you are not gifted enough, smart enough, talented enough, or qualified enough to engage in effective ministry. This is simply not true. You have the Word of God before you, the Spirit of God in you, and the command of God to you: make disciples of all nations. So whether you are a businessman or a businesswoman, a lawyer or a doctor, a consultant or a construction worker, a teacher or a student, an on-the-go professional or an on-the-go stay-at-home mom, I implore you to ask God to make your life count where you live for the spread of the gospel and the declaration of his glory to the ends of the earth.

A BETTER WAY

A house church leader in Asia once wrote how persecution in his country had stripped his church of its resources. Yet, in his mind, this had been a good thing. "We soon found that rather than being weakened by the removal of all external props, we were actually much stronger because our faith in God was purer," he wrote. "We didn't have any opportunity to love the 'things' of God, so we just learned to love God! We had no plans or programs to keep running, so we just sought the face of Jesus!... We don't believe the world needs another single church building. They need Jesus, and they need to worship and grow in God's grace with other believers...according to the pattern of the first church in the New Testament." Then this house church leader concluded, "When we finally reach the end of all our useless programs and give up in desperation, Jesus will always be there to show us a better way— his way."[14]

This is the beauty of the plan of God, particularly when we contrast it with the plans we create that are dependent on performances, places, programs, and professionals. If the spread of the gospel is dependent on these things, we will never reach the ends of the earth. We will never have enough resources, staff, buildings, events, or activities to reach all the people in our community, much less all the peoples in the world.

But we will always have enough people. Even if they seem like the wrong people.

If eleven disciples on a mountain in Galilee were enough to launch the gospel to the ends of the earth, then a church with a handful of members can spread the gospel in and beyond a community, regardless of the amount of material resources it has. The plan of God is certainly not confined to large churches or gifted leaders. The plan of God is for every person among the people of God to count for the advancement of the kingdom of God.

What if each of us were actually making disciples who were making disciples who were making disciples? Is it too idealistic to dream that the church of God, unleashed for the purpose of God, might actually reach the ends of the earth with the gospel? Is that realistic? You bet it is. In fact, it's guaranteed. Jesus has promised that every nation, tribe, tongue, and people are going to hear the gospel, and it is going to happen through all of us.[15]

CHAPTER FIVE

OUR UNMISTAKABLE
TASK

> WE ARE LIVING—AND LONGING—
> FOR THE END OF THE WORLD.

I was sitting in a small room on the most unevangelized island on earth. As I looked out the window, I saw the sun rising over shanties that spread across the landscape for miles. The mist began to disappear over the millions of men and women who inhabited this massive city in the middle of the island. Beyond the city limits, multitudes of other people were spread throughout rural villages, many of which require days of travel to reach.

As I watched the city begin to awaken, I heard the early morning call to prayer. Religious incantations resounded from loudspeakers stationed throughout the city so that everyone could hear them. Everywhere people began their day by solemnly going to prayer rooms and sacred sites to bow and worship.

Most of the forty-five million people on the island are Muslim, and most of them have never heard the gospel. Nearly fifty different people groups on the island have no church to speak of in their midst. Many of the people have never known a person who has confessed faith in Christ.

What is interesting, though, and unfortunately ironic, is that the most unevangelized island on earth is also home to millions of Christians. One of the largest tribes on the island is filled with professing believers. I wrote about them in *Radical*.

Years ago a Baptist couple came to this island to share the gospel with the tribal leaders. Those leaders did not like what they heard, and so they killed—and cannibalized—the two missionaries. Years later a Lutheran from Germany came to the same tribe. This time, when he proclaimed the gospel, the tribal leaders listened and believed. Within months the majority of the tribe had professed faith in Christ.

The problem, however, is that in the years since their mass conversion to Christianity, this tribe has turned inward. Due to a variety of factors, including cultural isolation and religious persecution, these Christians have virtually kept Christ to themselves.

Take the issue of pork. Muslim tribes across this island do not eat pork because they believe it is unclean. This Christian tribe, on the other hand, loves to eat pork. Naturally, any Christian wanting to reach Muslims with the gospel would be wise to abstain from pork around Muslims. Yet most Christians here are not willing to take even this small step. One believer succinctly said to a friend of mine on the island, "I would rather a Muslim go to hell than for me to have to stop eating pork."

Reaching Muslims here would not only be uncomfortable for Christians; it would also be costly. Many Muslim tribes on this island are devout, and one state practices shari'ah law. Anyone caught trying to lead people to Christ in that state will be imprisoned or likely even killed. Any Muslim caught converting to faith in Christ in that state will immediately be executed. Indeed, the price is high for any believer here who desires to engage the unreached with the gospel.

And so the Christians sit back. They are living next to multitudes of unreached peoples, yet they are unwilling to share Christ with them. Instead, they focus on church activities among themselves. They have constructed large church buildings all over the city. They have numerous denominational conventions, nearly thirty theological seminaries, and even mission boards organized among themselves throughout the island. My friend who lives here said, "David, they have all the trappings of the church. The only thing they are missing is the heart of Christ."

As soon as my friend said this, I was stunned into silence. I thought, *Is it really possible to have all the trappings of the church and yet miss the heart of Christ? Is it possible for church people to be so focused on personal comforts and so fearful of the potential cost that they virtually forget the purpose of God among all the peoples of the world?*

As I asked the questions, I realized the answers. Of course this is possible. Much of what we have seen in American Christianity proves it. We have massive resources, megabuildings, multitudes of programs, and a myriad of conferences and activities. Meanwhile, thousands of people groups around us in the world still haven't even heard the gospel. From most appearances in the church, however, we seem to be okay with that. We seem content to let these people groups continue church-less, Christ-less, and gospel-less. To seriously engage them with the gospel would be uncomfortable and costly.

That day when my friend told me about the attitude of the Christian tribespeople on the island, I looked at the city that surrounded me, and I wondered some more. *What if things were different here?* I thought. *What if this Christian tribe was willing to take some risks? What if they were willing to change their lifestyles in order to seriously engage the unreached on this island? What if their churches were willing to sacrifice their resources in order to creatively extend the gospel to people who have never heard it? Could every one of these people groups be penetrated for the glory of Christ?*

And that's when I begin to realize that the same potential resides in the church in my context. God has given great grace to the church I lead and to many other churches like it. He has given us vast resources, varied gifts, innumerable skills, immeasurable talents, and billions of dollars. If we were willing to take some risks, if we were willing to alter our lifestyles, and if we were willing to organize our churches around taking the gospel to people who have never heard of Christ, we could see every people group on the planet reached with the gospel. And in the process, we could be a part of the end of the world.

PEOPLE GROUPS

The end of the world?

Absolutely. That's what we're living—and longing—for. Now, before you think I've lost it, let me explain.

One day Jesus was having a conversation with his disciples

about the end of human history when he will come back. His discussion with the disciples on that day has sparked all kinds of debate since then about what he meant. Yet tucked away in the middle of a host of interpretive quagmires is a verse that is crystal clear. It is a statement that New Testament scholar George Eldon Ladd called "perhaps the most important single verse in the Word of God for God's people today."[1] As recorded in Matthew 24:14, Jesus said to his disciples, "This gospel of the kingdom will be preached in the whole world as a testimony to all nations, and then the end will come."

Here Jesus uses the same phrase that he would use later when commanding his followers not just to make disciples but to make disciples "of all nations."[2] *Nations* in the original language of the New Testament is *ethne*. It refers to all the ethnic peoples of the world.

This is important because, obviously, at the time Jesus said these words, the geopolitical boundaries that divide nations in our day didn't exist. More than 190 nations exist in the world today, but that is not what Jesus is referring to. When Jesus talks about the nations, he is talking about clans, tribes, and other groups of people united by common languages and cultural characteristics. Scholars have translated this term as "ethnolinguistic groups" or more simply as "people groups."

This makes sense, because one nation may be composed of many different people groups. Take India for example. India is a country made up of a diverse array of people groups with different languages and customs and cultures and religions. Numerous people groups are spread across India.

Anthropological experts have identified more than eleven thousand people groups in the world. We can't be sure that their definition of people groups squares precisely with what Jesus had in mind when he referred to *ethne,* but they offer our best estimate. Regardless of how one defines people groups, though, the reality is that in Matthew 28:19 Jesus specifically tells his disciples to go to all the world's people groups, and in Matthew 24:14 he promises that all of them will hear the gospel. Indeed, he is not coming back until all of them have heard.

I wonder if many of us have missed something very important here. Let me rephrase that: in countless studies and sermons on the Great Commission, *I* have missed something very important here. What we need to understand is that Jesus did not command us simply to take the gospel to as many individual people as we can. Instead, he made it clear that his followers are to make disciples *among every people group in the world.* The end of the age will not come when a certain number of people in one ethnic group come to Christ. The end of the age will come when people from every single ethnic group have come to Christ.

This has been God's plan from the beginning. He blessed Abraham and the people of Israel with the specific purpose of bringing his blessing to all people groups. He brought his children out of slavery in Egypt and settled them in the Promised Land for the purpose of his praise among all people groups. He sent them into exile and brought them out of exile in order to spread his glory among all people groups. Jesus promised that the gospel would be preached to all the people groups. The story of the church is the story of the spread of the gospel toward every people group, and leaders in the early church possessed consuming ambitions "to preach the gospel where Christ was not known."[3]

The apostle John puts an exclamation point on God's passion for praise from among all people groups when he records the song resounding from heaven to Jesus in the book of Revelation.

> I looked and there before me was a great multitude that no one could count, from every nation, tribe, people and language, standing before the throne and in front of the Lamb.... And they cried out in a loud voice:
>
> > "Salvation belongs to our God,
> > who sits on the throne,
> > and to the Lamb."[4]

There it is. In the end, just as God planned before time began, every ethnic group will be represented around the throne of Jesus, exalting his name and having received his salvation. In anticipation of that day, John closes the Bible by crying, "Come, Lord Jesus."[5]

He will come when every people group has heard the gospel. For this reason he has charged his church, not just generally with getting the gospel to as many people as we can, but specifically with getting the gospel to every people group on this planet. Indeed, he is not coming back until this assignment has been accomplished.

You might be wondering what amount of work is yet to be

done. Well, mission leaders around the world have tried to identify which people groups are still unreached with the gospel. According to their definitions, a people group is classified as unreached if less than 2 percent of the population is made up of evangelical Christians. This means that if you are a part of an unreached people group, likely you will be born, you will live, and you will die without ever hearing the gospel. And out of more than eleven thousand people groups in the world, *more than six thousand of them* are still unreached.

Our task, therefore, is massive and unmistakable. Thousands of people groups have not yet been reached with the gospel, and Jesus has commanded (not merely *called* but *commanded*) us to get the gospel to them. So for you and me not to be intentionally engaged in taking the gospel to unreached people groups is disobedience to the command of Christ. Our churches are in the wrong before God if we are not prioritizing the spread of the gospel to every people group.

"Well," some might object, "what if the way we define people groups is not how Jesus defines people groups? And what if our definition of 'reached' is not the same as his? Are you saying that Jesus won't or can't come back tomorrow because there's still more than six thousand people groups (as we've defined them) who have yet to be reached (as we've defined that) with the gospel?"

I want to be careful here, for as I have already admitted, our definitions of unreached people groups may not be exact. The reality is that Jesus could come back as I write (or as you read) this sentence, and not one of us knows the time when he will come.[6]

But we do know this: Jesus hasn't come back yet, which means there is still work to be done.

I can't improve on George Ladd's words at this point. He wrote:

> God alone knows the definition of terms. I cannot precisely define who "all the nations" are. Only God knows exactly the meaning of "evangelize." He alone…will know when that objective has been accomplished. But I do not need to know. I know only one thing: Christ has not yet returned; therefore the task is not yet done. When it is done, Christ will come. Our responsibility is not to insist on defining the terms of our task; our responsibility is to complete it. So long as Christ does not return, our work is undone. Let us get busy and complete our mission.[7]

this explains why islam is on the rise so fast — its satan's attempt to keep Jesus from coming back

THE BATTLE OVER THE PEOPLES

When I first began to realize the weight of what Jesus was expressing in Matthew 24:14—"This gospel of the kingdom will be preached in the whole world as a testimony to all nations, and then the end will come"—I immediately thought, *Satan must have this verse plastered all over the walls of hell as a warning!* Why? Because when all the people groups of the world have been reached with the gospel and the end comes, that's not good news for the forces of evil. For Satan and his demons, the end spells eternal doom. Without question, then, Satan is working feverishly with all the resources at his disposal to prevent the day when the gospel will be preached to all people groups. <u>He does not want the end to come.</u>

<u>The question is, do we?</u> Do we want to see our Savior surrounded by a throng of representatives from every nation, tribe, language, and people giving him the glory he is due?

If we do want the end to come, it will cost us. Right before Jesus gave the promise in Matthew 24:14, he said, "You will be handed over to be persecuted and put to death, and you will be hated by all nations because of me."[8] The reason so many people groups are still unreached is not because they are easy to reach and we just haven't had the resources to get them the gospel. They are unreached because they are hard to reach and we haven't had the resolve to get them the gospel. Any Christian and any church desiring to obey the command of Christ in the world and longing to see the coming of Christ at the end of the world must possess a God-centered, gospel-driven tenacity that is ready to endure an intense spiritual battle.

The scope of this spiritual battle is universal. And because it encompasses every tongue, tribe, language, and nation, there is no place on this planet where the war will not be waged.

The stakes in this spiritual battle are eternal. There is a true God over this world who desires all peoples to experience everlasting joy in heaven. And there is a false god in this world who desires all peoples to experience everlasting suffering in hell.

Our enemy in this spiritual battle is formidable. He is like a lion looking for his kill, and he is dead set on defaming God and destroying us. Where the church exists, he works to discourage us with trials and temptations. He lures us with possessions and prosperity, and he lulls us with comforts and complacency. He does everything he can to distract the church from knowing Christ and declaring his glory to the ends of the earth.

And his tactics are subtle; we could even say missional. Amid much talk in the church today about being missional, the Adversary may subtly be deceiving our minds about mission. We are exhorted to see ourselves as missionaries in our cities, and we are encouraged to engage our cultures with the gospel. These exhortations and encouragements are needed correctives for church mind-sets that have compartmentalized and limited mission. But, biblically, our mission is not only about loving our city or invading our culture with the gospel. Our mission is also about leaving our cities to infiltrate every culture with the gospel. I am convinced that Satan, in a sense, is just fine with missional churches in the West spending the overwhelming majority of our time, energy, and money on trying to reach people right around us. Satan may actually delight in this, for while we spend our lives on the people we see in front of us, more than six thousand people groups for generations have never even heard the gospel and remain in the dark.

But when we rise up as the church of Jesus Christ and give ourselves urgently, sacrificially, and radically to taking the gospel of the kingdom to all those people groups, we can expect to be met with the might of hell. There will be divisions within us, distractions around us, diversions in front of us, deceptions tempting us, and disease and death threatening us. It will not be easy. And it will cost. However, truly missional churches and truly missional

Christians will set their sights on the world, and they will over-come the Adversary "by the blood of the Lamb and by the word of their testimony" because they do "not love their lives so much as to shrink from death."[9]

BROOK HILLS BARUTI

If the ultimate goal of the church is to take the gospel to all peo-ple groups, then everything we do in the church must be aimed toward that end.

When I came to Brook Hills, I was encouraged to identify our target audience. "Who is Brook Hills Bob?" I was asked. In other words, what was the profile of the person we were most try-ing to reach?

The profile seemed obvious. Businesspeople fill our commu-nity. Their average age is in the forties, and they have good edu-cations and well-paying jobs that enable them to support families with multiple children in an upper-middle-class community. This sort of person, some would say, is who we need to focus on as a church.

I disagree.

It's not that I think Brook Hills Bob is unimportant. He's extremely important, and we want men and women like that and their families in Birmingham to come to Christ. But we decided our goal was not to reach Brook Hills Bob. Instead, our target was going to be Brook Hills Baruti.

Let me explain. Baruti doesn't live in our community. Instead, he lives thousands of miles away in North Africa. He is illiterate and poorly paid. He attempts to survive on meager daily rations of food and water from outside sources. He was born into a spiritually and physically impoverished people group where almost no one knows Jesus or has even heard of him. And Baruti's people like it that way. When a woman in Baruti's people group heard about Christ and trusted in him for salvation, she was immediately killed—by her husband and her father. Baruti fervently worships a false god and is blinded to the reality of his sin and resistant to the message of a Savior.

That's who we are setting out to reach at Brook Hills. We are going to live and plan and strategize and organize and work so that Baruti hears and receives the gospel.

This changes everything about how we do ministry at Brook Hills. If our goal is all nations, then our strategy cannot be defined by what will best reach people within ten miles of our church building. If our goal is all nations, then our strategy must always revolve around what will best reach people who are ten thousand miles from our church building.

This doesn't mean we neglect Brook Hills Bob or anyone else who is right around us. Indeed, we are going to reach Bob and all kinds of other people in our community. But as they come to Christ, we are going to encourage them to spend their lives spreading the gospel to Baruti. We're going to teach them to pray for Baruti and the billion other people like him who don't have the gospel. We're going to train them to know God's Word so they will be ready to share it on the spot in our culture and in other cultures. We're going to encourage them to stop using their resources for more comforts in Birmingham and start using their resources to get the gospel to people like Baruti. We're going to dream with them about how they can leverage their businesses, their relationships, and the positions, possessions, influence, wealth, gifts, and talents that God has given them for the sake of God's glory in Baruti's life. We're going to mobilize them to make disciples in simple, reproducible, cross-cultural ways here that will one day impact Baruti over there.

Someone might say, "It sounds like Bob is just a means to an end and Baruti is the end. Are you saying that Baruti is somehow more important, or more valuable, than Bob?" That's a great question, and that's not at all what I am saying. Bob and Baruti are equally valued by God and equally lost without God. They both need the gospel. But if the church I lead focuses only on Bob, then even if we are successful in reaching Bob, we will ultimately be disobedient to Jesus' command to get the gospel to all people groups, including Baruti's people group. Therefore, I want to make sure that the church I lead has its sights set on Baruti, not to the exclusion of Bob, but to the inclusion of Bob and everyone else in Birmingham. And once we reach Baruti together, we will equip Baruti to reach still other unreached people. And we won't stop until the word *unreached* is no longer applicable to any people group!

NOT EITHER/OR BUT BOTH/AND

This is part of the genius of making disciples. When we follow the pattern and precedent of Jesus, we will never have to choose whether to impact Bob *or* to impact Baruti. We will always be living for the spread of the gospel to Bob *and* Baruti.

Consider the life and leadership of Jesus. Surely he had a passion for the glory of the Father in all nations. Yet he spent his life with a small group of men in a relatively isolated geographic area. His ministry to them, however, was always for the purpose of the spread of the gospel beyond them. Jesus didn't care only about needs in Jerusalem or Galilee. He cared about the nations so deeply that he poured his life into a handful of men in Jerusalem and Galilee who would one day turn the world upside down.[10] Jesus cared so much about getting the gospel to Americans in the twenty-first century that he poured his life into twelve Jewish men in the first century. It was never an either/or for Jesus; it was always a both/and.

We and our churches never have to choose between impacting people with the gospel locally and impacting them globally. Disciple making frees us from having to make that choice. As we lay down our lives to multiply the gospel in the context of intentional relationships where we live, we are always doing it ultimately for the spread of the gospel far beyond where we live. And if we are faithful to Jesus' command in the Great Commission, we will always be living and longing for the spread of the gospel to all people groups.

Consider Jack and Sarah, a couple in our faith family. In many ways Jack would fit the profile of Brook Hills Bob. He is a successful, middle-aged businessman living in Birmingham. When Jack and Sarah came to faith in Christ, they began inviting other couples into their home, where they helped these husbands and wives come to Christ and grow in Christ. After a time of intentional investment in these couples, Jack and Sarah began sending them out of their home to start making disciples on their own. Meanwhile, Jack and Sarah found new couples to invest their lives in.

But their story goes deeper. Jack and Sarah understand that disciple making is the avenue for the accomplishment of the global purpose of God. So Jack began mobilizing his business and leveraging his assets to be a part of spreading the gospel in spiritually and physically impoverished places around the world. Then, in the context of their relationships with other couples in their home, Jack and Sarah began leading these other families to do the same thing in their spheres of influence. As a part of this process, Jack and Sarah have taken these couples overseas on short-term mission trips to expose them to God's heart for the world, and then Jack and Sarah have challenged each of them to consider how their lives and families can be used for the spread of the gospel in the world.

Because they are making disciples, the fruit of Jack's and Sarah's lives is unmistakably local *and* global. Though they live in the same place where they have lived for the last twenty years, their home has become a ministry base to the world. Some of the couples who have been discipled by Jack and Sarah now live in low-income communities in Birmingham, where they are investing in people in the same way Jack and Sarah invested in them. Other couples have moved overseas. We currently have couples living in Africa and Asia who were impacted by the disciple making of Jack and Sarah. Some of the other couples who have shared life with Jack and Sarah haven't moved anywhere, but they are spending their lives making disciples and using their resources for the spread of the gospel to the ends of the earth, just as they've seen in Jack and Sarah.

Jack has never asked me, "Pastor, why don't we care about people in Birmingham?" because he realizes that true disciple making in Birmingham will have an impact on the nations with the gospel and vice versa. For Jack and Sarah, the plan of God is never about ministering here or among the nations. For Jack and Sarah, the plan of God is always about ministering here for the sake of the nations. By the way, one of the couples that Jack and Sarah discipled is now leading our church-planting team that serves among an unreached people group in North Africa.

Brook Hills Bob has been reached for the sake of Brook Hills Baruti.

SHORT-TERM MISSIONS
WITH LONG-TERM IMPACT

This is part of the reason I am a strong believer in short-term mission trips. I can talk until I am blue in the face about setting our sights on the nations, but until someone actually goes and sees the nations in person, he or she is likely to underestimate the urgency of God's global purpose in our lives. For this reason, at Brook Hills we are intentional about encouraging people in the church to take concentrated time every year possible to go into another context and spread the gospel.

We hear many criticisms of short-term missions, and some are valid. Short-term mission trips are often nothing more than glorified vacations. They can be sightseeing tours filled with sporadic service opportunities that give people an opportunity to pat themselves on the back while doing little to advance the gospel in a reproducible, sustainable way in another culture.

Successful short-term missions must be a part of fueling a long-term disciple-making process in another context. Clearly, no one is going to make disciples in another country over the span of one week. To expect to make disciples in just a few days is both impractical and unbiblical. However, we can partner with believers in other contexts who are intentionally making disciples, and our time serving alongside them can help move their disciple-making processes along in exponential ways.

At the same time, successful short-term missions must also be a part of fueling long-term disciple making in the sending church. As we go together into other contexts, we grow together in Christ. Our eyes are opened and our hearts are transformed as we serve in situations that make us uncomfortable. Whether we're serving impoverished brothers and sisters or sharing the gospel with people who have never heard it before, God does a work in our hearts that will not leave us unchanged. Part of the purpose of short-term missions is to walk through situations like this alongside others who will help us, challenge us, serve us, and spur us on toward Christ in the midst of it all.

I remember one trip to Tegucigalpa, Honduras. I had been on mission trips before, but this one was different. We were working with a church that was making disciples in the midst of extreme poverty, and nothing could have prepared me for what I saw on a mountainside one day.

As we came over a ridge on the outskirts of this sprawling city,

my eyes beheld seemingly endless hills covered with piles of smol-
dering trash. My nose burned with the smell of household waste
and human excrement. For most of the people in the region, this
place was known as the city dump. For an unfortunate few,
though, this place was known as home.

When we walked into the dump, we discovered makeshift
houses made of sticks and plastic tarps nestled in the piles of trash.
Families lived here—men, women, and children—whose suste-
nance each day depended on finding a livelihood in the stench of
others' leftovers. I will never forget seeing a young girl of maybe
five or six years standing knee deep in the garbage she called her
front yard.

As we worked atop that mountain, we served alongside the
local church and learned what it means to love people on their
own turf. At the same time, a man who had come on that trip
helped me process what was taking place. And on that day it
clicked for me. All the statistics about hundreds of millions in desperate poverty, all the facts about men, women, and children dying
from preventable diseases or lack of food and water, and all the
truths I had resisted came crashing down on my heart. I realized
that the rest of my life must be different.

In light of the potential and power of short-term missions in
long-term disciple making both here and around the world, every
year we challenge every member of our faith family to give 2 percent of his or her time (which works out to be about a week) in
some other context outside of Birmingham to spread the gospel.
We relationally connect with disciple making taking place in other
contexts while we intentionally focus on the disciple-making

processes in our church. In this way, that 2 percent of our time in another context ends up radically changing the 98 percent of our time in our own community. As one church member put it, "My time overseas has transformed my time across the street."

LONG-TERM MISSION FROM SHORT-TERM IMPACT

The inevitable result of short-term missions done right is radically changed lives. Some from our church have returned to say, "I believe God is calling me to spend 98 percent of my time in another context and come back to my current context for a 2 percent visit each year." In this way, short-term mission trips end up fueling long-term commitments.

For example, in the last month we have commissioned a journalist, a teacher, and a businessman to move overseas. Over the last year we have sent out a diverse group of disciple makers, from an engineer to a school administrator. Some are going through traditional avenues, others through unconventional ones. Some are going through mission organizations, others through business platforms.

Recently a couple told us, "We don't really see ourselves as missionaries. We're just Christians with transferable job skills who thought, Why not work in Asia and live out the gospel there among people who have never heard of Jesus?" That's a great question, and I praise God for how people are answering it all across the church.

We are currently in the process of sending teams of students and senior adults, businesspeople and church planters, who will work together to see churches planted and disciples made among those who have never heard the gospel. Every time we prepare to send a team, I challenge every member of the church (myself included) to ask God if he desires for us to go and then to wait for an answer. God can be trusted with these kinds of prayers from his people, and he will be faithful to provide those he leads with everything they need to accomplish the task he puts before them.

As I share these stories from our faith family, I want to say clearly that we are not doing things perfectly. These past few years have been filled with some incredible joys as we have engaged the world, but we have also experienced some discouraging struggles. At times we have jumped too fast into opportunities overseas, and at other times we have moved too slowly. We have a long way to go and a lot more to learn about how to most effectively make disciples in other contexts. But we're not going to stop. We want to see the unreached reached with the gospel.

I know you desire the same thing. Who could imagine the impact if a few thousand churches decided to pray for, give to, and go to just one or two unreached people groups apiece? Consider what would happen if each of our churches adopted (or a couple of churches joined together and adopted) an unreached people group and decided to organize an intentional strategy for leveraging the resources of the church here for the spread of the gospel there. This is the plan of God—penetrating every nation with the gospel—and he has promised to bless it! If we are obedient to his plan, could we not see the accomplishment of the Great Commission in our day? Is this not worth the sacrifice of our lives and our churches?

THE GOSPEL FOR ALL

I was born into a context where the gospel of Jesus is relatively accessible. I have heard about Jesus' death on the cross practically since the day I was born. I am overwhelmed whenever I think about where I would be without the gospel. And I am humbled when I consider that I had nothing to do with where I was born. The only reason I have heard the gospel of God is because of the grace of God.

Meanwhile, more than six thousand people groups equaling nearly two billion people still do not have access to the gospel. For generations they and their ancestors have been born, have lived, and have died without even hearing the name of Jesus. I am even more humbled when I consider that they had nothing to do with where they were born either.

So why have I heard the message of the gospel when they have not? Why have I received such mercy from God? This question is not just for me but for all who live where the gospel is accessible and who participate in churches where the gospel is abundant. Why have we been given such immeasurable grace when none of us has done anything to deserve it?

I do not presume to know all of God's motives, but I will propose this: you and I have been given the great mercy of God for a global mission from God. He has called, commissioned, and commanded each of us as Christians to give ourselves to the spread of his gospel in every part of the earth. All nations, all tribes, all language groups, and all peoples will one day hear this news, and then the end will come. As a result, every church that passionately loves the gospel of Christ and patiently longs for the coming of Christ will purposefully live for the glory of Christ among those who have never heard his name.

We are living—and longing—for the end of the world.

CHAPTER SIX

THE GOD WHO EXALTS GOD

WE ARE SELFLESS FOLLOWERS
OF A SELF-CENTERED GOD.

After the release of *Radical,* people from different churches began e-mailing me to share how Christ was calling them to radical obedience.

Jacob and Stephanie were storing up money for a bigger house when they began considering the claims of Christ upon their lives. In their words, "We realized we were working toward worldly goals, so we began praying that God would open our eyes to his plan, even if it meant letting go of our dreams." As they prayed, the Lord drew their attention to children with Down syndrome in need of adoption. Said Stephanie, "As I looked at hundreds of faces of children in need [on a Web site], tears poured down, and I knew that we were not supposed to build a bigger home but to give a home to one of these children."

Together, they have begun the process of adopting a child

with Down syndrome. As for the larger home, they actually went in the opposite direction, selling the home they had to move into a smaller one. That will free up more of their resources for God's purposes. Stephanie wrote, "I can't believe how God is transforming our lives. Instead of Christianity being a chore or a legalistic to-do list, it's a relationship. I wake up every day eager to hear more from God. I'm reading the Bible as if it's the first time I've ever picked it up. I regret that I have wasted so much of my life living for myself, but I'm not wasting it anymore. I cannot wait to see where God takes us from here!"

Jacob and Stephanie are joined by many other church members I have talked to who are rearranging their lifestyles, reorganizing their families, and reallocating their resources to make their lives count for the global purpose of God. Some of them are staying in the United States. Others are moving overseas.

Melissa described her feelings when her husband, Mark, approached her about downsizing their home. "When Mark initially suggested that we should move out of our posh loft and look into living somewhere that costs significantly less, I balked. 'Um, Mark,' I said, 'we use this loft for Jesus.' Apparently that wasn't good enough, and he continued to gently 'suggest' in the days ahead. God began changing my heart as I began to discover all the other things I was holding on to 'for Jesus.' Funny, Jesus didn't hold on to anything that was rightfully his but made himself nothing, taking the very nature of a servant." Compelled by the gospel, Mark and Melissa have moved into a low-income community where they are sharing and showing the gospel while "furthering

God's kingdom with the money, resources, and time that he has given us."

Tom and Amy took a different step. Amy wrote, "I grew up in a little town in Texas and have never lived more than two hours from my family. But the gospel is compelling us to forsake our comforts, our family, and our home in order to follow God into the unknown. Along with our two daughters, we will follow wherever he leads." God is now leading Tom, Amy, and their family to move to Prague. Amy reports that they are learning to "depend on him to accomplish his goal—the spreading of the gospel in one of the most openly atheistic countries in Europe."

Obviously, moving from one place to another is not the only possible application of Christ's commands in our lives. His words are playing out in different ways in people from different places.

Jorge is a postal service retiree from a church in Arizona, and God has led him to begin gospel ministry with fellow Hispanics in his community.

Christine is a stay-at-home mom from a church in Washington State, and she has started a ministry to Christian teachers working in third-world countries.

Lauren is a college senior from a church in London, and she's planning to use her studies and skills to work among people who have never heard of Christ.

DeShawn is a high school junior from a church in Florida, and he has organized outreach opportunities for his peers to participate in sharing the gospel around his community every Sunday.

Stan is the pastor of a church in North Carolina, and he

recently went before his congregation to (in his words) "publicly repent for just doing church and for being unconcerned about the nations." He is now leading them "to share the gospel, serve the poor, and shake the nations."

Why?

Why are local churches beginning to reshape their priorities and reassess their spending in light of urgent spiritual and physical needs around the world? And why are their members changing their lifestyles, packing their bags, selling their homes, moving to low-income areas, or taking their families to dangerous places? It is certainly not because they read an orange book entitled *Radical*. Rather, it is because they are gripped by an overwhelming God. They know they belong to a God who desires, deserves, and demands absolute devotion in their lives and in their churches, and they want to give him nothing less. He is worthy of their all—their lives, their budgets, their ambitions, their programs, their relationships, their possessions, their careers, and their trust.

As Christians joined together with one another in the church, we are selfless followers of a self-centered God. We are selfless in that we have died to ourselves. We have lost the right to determine the direction of our lives. Our God is our Lord, our Master, and our King. He holds our times in his hands, and he is free to spend our lives however he pleases. And he is self-centered. In his Word, God declares his own glory, and in the world, God displays his own glory. God exalts God. If this rubs us wrong in any way, we should ask, "Who else would we have him exalt?" For at the very moment God exalts anyone or anything else, he is no longer the God who is worthy of all exaltation. Everything God does, even the salvation of his people, ultimately centers around God, for he is worthy of all praise from all peoples.[1]

So it's really true that, individually and together, we are to be selfless followers of a self-centered God. But the problem is that we often reverse this in the church. We become self-centered followers of a selfless God. We organize our churches as if God exists to meet our needs, cater to our comforts, and appeal to our preferences. Discussions in the church more often revolve around what we want than what he wills. Almost unknowingly, the church becomes a means of self-entertainment and a monument to self-sufficiency. But something wonderful happens when we apply radical obedience to Christ in the regular practice of the church. All of a sudden, we find ourselves engulfed in a community that finds deep and abiding pleasure in denial of self and dependence on God.

LOSING OUR LIVES OR SIPPING OUR LATTES?

I spent my first few months as a pastor in a steep learning curve. Because I had never pastored before, I devoured books on how to determine and communicate a vision for where a church is going. In order to lead your church anywhere, these books told me, you need a preferred future, a visual destination, for which you are working. Pastors I respect declared, "Decide how big you want your church to be, and go for it, whether that's five, ten, or twenty thousand members. Envision what your church campus (or multiple campuses) will look like five, ten, or twenty years from now,

and start working toward it. Dream about how your worship services can become more innovative. All of this is important, so consider hiring a creative consultant to help you craft your vision.
After all, Proverbs 29:18 says that where there is no vision, the
people will perish."[2]

At first it seemed to make sense. But over time I found myself
getting nauseated by all the vision talk. Setting and reaching goals
is important, of course. But were my sights really supposed to be
set on bringing a large crowd together in a cool environment
where they could hear terrific music, see killer graphics, and then
listen to me talk live or via video or maybe even via hologram (if
only I had really innovative vision)? If this was to be the vision of
my life and ministry, I decided, then I should perish.

So I sat down with members in our church, and together we
asked, "What is our vision? What do we want to see? Where do
we want to fasten our attention in the days to come? What do we
want to work toward with all our hearts?"

As we prayed together, the answer became obvious. The only
possible vision for the church of Jesus Christ is to make known the
glory of God in all nations. This preferred future or visual destination must drive us because this is what drives God. Far more
than we want stuff for the church, crowds at the church, or activities in the church, we want to know, love, honor, and praise God.
And we want all people to do the same. We want to see God glorified by people everywhere because God wants to see himself glorified by people everywhere.

Vision affects everything. That's what visions do. If the focus
of the church is on having a large crowd in a big place where peo-

ple can come and feel warm and welcomed, then you and I will plan accordingly. We will prioritize a nice church campus for people to drive to and where they can find a convenient parking space. We'll give them a latte when they walk in the door, and then we'll provide state-of-the-art entertainment for their children while treating them to a great show that leaves them feeling good when they drive away in a timely fashion. Variations of this vision engineered for the savvy Christian consumer are multiplied across the landscape of our country today, and they work well. The crowds come, and the vision is realized.

But what happens when our vision changes? What happens when our primary aim is not to make the crowds feel comfortable but to exalt God in all his glory? Suddenly our priorities begin to change. More than you and I want people to be impressed by the stuff we can manufacture, we want them to be amazed by the God they cannot fathom. More than we want to dazzle them with our production, we want to direct them to his praise. And the last thing we want to do is raise up people who are casual in the worship of God as they sit back and enjoy their lattes. Instead, we want to raise up people who are so awed, so captivated, so mesmerized by the glory of God that they will gladly lose their lattes—and their lives—to make his greatness known in the world.

RADICALLY SEEKER SENSITIVE

"But what's so wrong with the lattes?" someone might ask. "Isn't it good to cater creatively to people who don't know God? Don't we want to be sensitive to those who are seeking God?"

Great questions. As you and I think about all the people who are without Christ in our communities, we long to see as many of them as possible come to Christ. Without question, we want to do everything we can to see people saved.

. But let me remind you of a startling reality that the Bible makes clear: "There is…no one who seeks God."[3] So if the church is sensitive to seekers, and if no one is seeking God, then that means the church is sensitive to no one. That's radical, but probably not the kind of radical we're looking for.

Instead, Jesus tells us that the Father is pursuing worshipers for his praise.[4] *He* is the one doing the seeking! He has been seeking sinners for thousands of years, and he is pretty good at it—far better than all the attractions and allurements we can assemble. So since you and I want to see people come to Christ in the church, let's do everything we can to put the wonders of God's glory, holiness, wrath, justice, kindness, jealousy, grace, and character on display in his church. Let's show people the most biblical, holistic, clear, and captivating vision of God that we possibly can and then trust him to take care of the seeking.

I think about Eric, who came to our church one Sunday at the request of his parents. He was addicted to drugs and had almost lost his life as a result. At the end of himself, he walked into our worship gathering, where we sang songs about God's greatness and studied Scripture about God's glory. In 1 Corinthians 14, Paul tells what will happen when an unbeliever comes into a worship gathering of the church: "He will be convinced by all [he is hearing] that he is a sinner and will be judged by all, and the secrets of his heart will be laid bare. So he will fall down and worship God, exclaiming, 'God is really among you!'"⁵ Well, Eric had a 1 Corinthians 14 moment that day. As he was captivated by the greatness of God in the church, he began to cry out for the grace of God in his life. Eric was saved from his sins that Sunday, not because he came seeking after God, but because God came seeking after him.

So let's be radically seeker sensitive in our churches. But let's make sure we are being sensitive to the right Seeker.

What Advances the Gospel

I know of no greater motivational tool for the church than a glimpse of the sovereign, holy, majestic God who is worthy of all worship, who is high and lifted up. This vision alone will compel a church to radical, risk-taking, death-defying obedience to the purpose of God in the world. For when our faith communities actually believe that God deserves the praise of all peoples, then our humble worship in the church will lead to an urgent witness in the world.

When we see three thousand animistic tribes across Africa worshiping all kinds of suspicious spirits and false gods, we will be compelled to go to Africa and declare the glory of the one true God.

When we see countries like Japan, Laos, and Vietnam filled with 350 million people following Buddha's beliefs and practices, we will be compelled to go to those countries and proclaim the greatness of Christ above Buddha and everyone else.

When we see people in India, Nepal, Bangladesh, and Sri Lanka worshiping literally millions of gods in the name of Hinduism, then we will go to those countries and tell people that there is one God over all gods.

When we see over a billion people in communist environments around the world who possess an atheistic view of God, we will be compelled to go to China, Cuba, and North Korea to tell people that God does exist and that he deserves their praise.

When we see more than a billion Muslims in some of the toughest places in the world for a Christian to live, we will sacrifice our lives, if necessary, to go to them because we want the glory of God in all nations more than we want our own safety in this world.

I think of Moravian churches in early eighteenth-century Germany. Before William Carey ever sailed to India or Hudson Taylor ever landed in China, these brothers and sisters were pioneering Western involvement in the global purpose of God. And it was costly. Two Moravian believers decided to sell themselves into slavery in order to reach slaves in the Caribbean with the gospel. As their ship set sail for St. Thomas, these brothers were heard crying out, "Worthy is the Lamb to receive the reward of his suffering!" The worth of Christ compelled these men to lose their lives for witness in the world.

Then I think of Adoniram Judson, who believed God was leading him to spend his life spreading the gospel among people who had never heard it. He met Ann and fell in love with her, but he needed to ask Ann's father for permission to marry her. So Judson wrote him this letter:

I have now to ask, whether you can consent to part with
your daughter early next spring, to see her no more in this
world; whether you can consent to her departure, and her
subjection to the hardships and sufferings of a missionary
life; whether you can consent to her exposure to the dan-
gers of the ocean; to the fatal influence of the southern
climate of India; to every kind of want and distress; to
degradation, insult, persecution, and perhaps a violent
death. Can you consent to all this, for the sake of him
who left his heavenly home, and died for her and for you;
for the sake of perishing, immortal souls; for the sake of
Zion, and the glory of God? Can you consent to all this,
in hope of soon meeting your daughter in the world of
glory, with the crown of righteousness, brightened with
the acclamations of praise which shall redound to her
Savior from heathens saved, through her means, from
eternal woe and despair?[6]

The driving ambition behind Judson's appeal to his potential
father-in-law was the prospect of God being glorified in other
nations. His father-in-law approved, and in the end it did cost his
daughter her life. *only God can do this!*

During thirty-eight years overseas, Adoniram Judson lost two
wives and seven children to premature death. Yet today there are
nearly four thousand Baptist churches with over half a million followers of Christ in the heart of Buddhist Burma (Myanmar).
Adoniram and Ann Judson believed the worship of God was

*I can't even imagine it! So far to go! But
I can't. He must take me.*

worth their lives, and churches who sow this kind of passion in worship will inevitably send this kind of people into the world.

I think of the men and women I presently pastor.

I think of the single women we have sent to West Africa and the Middle East to work in some of the toughest contexts in the world. One of them, Jana, recently shared with the church, "God is not willing that any should perish, and neither am I. He wants all people to know him, and that's why I am going."

I think of entire families who have moved to a foreign country. Joseph is a doctor who took his wife and three children to work in the midst of spiritual and physical poverty overseas. He wrote me recently:

> I have frequently had to decide which of two critically ill patients gets the one available ICU bed. The ramification for the patient not chosen can be, and has been, deadly. Recently I had to sit across the table from a room full of family members and explain that their loved one—a mother of ten, including a newborn—would not be coming home. I am daily the object of impossible questions for which no attainable answers exist. I have life-and-death responsibilities in areas in which I have limited training. My wife and children struggle with social isolation, frequent good-byes, and distance from friends and family. No one said that coming here would be easy. No one said that following God would be easy. I didn't expect it to be, and indeed it is not.

He went on to say, "What these people need is an advocate who shares their burdens and knows their fear, and we cannot show the love of Jesus Christ to them without descending into the valley of the shadow of death with them. Indeed, that is what Jesus has done for us. And so that is what I endeavor to do, all the while trusting that God will be true to his promise and not task me with more than I am able to bear."

I think of Brandon and Lydia, a young couple whom our pastors recently interviewed as we prepare to send them into one of the most dangerous areas in the world. One of the pastors asked this precious wife, "Are you sure that you are ready for what lies ahead?"

The room fell silent as she softly responded, "I believe God's Word is true. His Word says that the gospel will advance through persecution and suffering. And I am good with that."

Nothing can stop a people who are trusting in the Word of God and living for the worship of God.

A CONSTANT DEPENDENCE

Unleashing God's people to accomplish God's purpose in the world requires that we devote ourselves to relentless prayer in the church. Why? Because prayer is one of the primary demonstrations of our selflessness and God's self-centeredness. In our selflessness, you and I realize that it is impossible for us to accomplish his purpose in our own strength. So we express our dependence upon God in prayer, and he delights in showing his glory by giving us everything we need for the accomplishment of his purpose. Through prayer, God gives grace to us in such a way that he receives glory for himself.

Prayer is a nonnegotiable priority for selfless followers of a self-centered God.

When you read the story of the early church in the book of Acts, you see people for whom prayer was fundamental, not supplemental. Three times Luke tells us that the church was devoted to prayer.[7] They were utterly dependent on God's power. Every major breakthrough for the church in the book of Acts came about as a direct result of prayer.[8] God performed mighty works for the propagation of the gospel and the declaration of his glory in direct proportion to the prayers of his people.

As the early church prayed, Luke tells us, "much grace was upon them all."[9] In the pages of Acts, we see the grace of God working powerfully through his people at every turn.[10] Every advance of the gospel message came, not by human innovation, but by divine visitation.

These believers knew that prayer was necessary for the accomplishment of God's purpose in the world. The point of prayer is not to carry on business as usual in the church. The reality is, we can conduct monotonous, human-centered religion on our own. But if we want to make disciples in all the nations, then we will need to pray. For when we sacrifice everything we are and stake everything we have on the front lines of a battle for the souls of millions of people around us and billions of people around the world who have little to no knowledge of Jesus, we are forced to pray.

I remember traveling to Sudan for the first time. Persecution and war were still prevalent in the region of southern Sudan where we were going, making it the most dangerous trip I had ever gone on. Even praying about the possibility of going was a challenge for my wife and me, but we were convinced it was God's will.

The team I went with arrived in Kenya and spent a couple of days there before going into Sudan. The night before we were to fly to Sudan, my friend who had organized the trip brought us all together and said, "There's a potential risk that we have not yet discussed, and we need to discuss it before we leave tomorrow morning."

Everybody got quiet.

"We know there are threats of bombings and raids in these villages," he explained. "But we also need to talk about the threat of snakes."

For the record, I'm not a big fan of snakes.

"You need to know," my friend continued, "that a majority of the deadliest snakes in the world live in Sudan." He began to name them—the green mamba, the black mamba, and so on. He described how lethal their bites are. Then he said, almost in jest, "If you get bit by one of these snakes, we have a snake kit, but it really won't do anything for these kinds of snakes. So if you get bit, we'll just pray and see what happens."

I was now considering the possibility that God, even though I had thought he wanted me to go to Sudan, really wanted me to stay in Kenya.

This possibility grew more appealing as my friend continued. "Last year," he said, "a Sudanese villager was walking his cattle down a path in the jungle, and a green mamba was hiding up in a tree. Suddenly it plunged down and bit a couple of his cows. The cows fell over dead within minutes."

I was frozen as I listened. A few minutes later he concluded our meeting and told us to get a good night's sleep so we'd be ready for the morning.

Yeah, right.

I tried to sleep that night, but every time I closed my eyes, I saw mambas. So instead of sleeping, I stayed up and memorized Psalm 91. Verse 13 says,

> You will tread upon the lion and the cobra;
> you will trample the great lion and the serpent.

I figured that if I didn't have anything else in the snake-ridden Sudanese jungle, I was at least going to have the Word with me.

The next day we rode a small plane for a few hours until we landed on a makeshift airstrip in the middle of Sudan. We got our bags and made our way to a river. It turned out that this was a crocodile-infested river, and we were crossing it in a canoe that some Sudanese had affectionately labeled on its side *The Mayfloat*.

Very funny.

So we crossed the crocodile-infested river in *The Mayfloat*, and we came to a Jeep on the other side. There was enough room for most of the guys to get inside the Jeep, but not all of us. Someone would need to ride on top. My friend asked if I'd be willing to go up there. I told him I would be glad to, and I climbed on top.

We began to move forward, I looked up, and all I saw were

trees everywhere. Immediately I thought of the green mamba story from the night before, and I panicked. What if a mamba like the one that bit the cows dropped on me?

I didn't have anywhere to go or anything to do. So I did all that I knew to do. I started speaking to the trees and any snakes therein: "You will trample upon the lion and the serpent! You will trample on the cobra!"

This set the stage for the whole trip. Everywhere we went, I was on the lookout. I would go to bed at night praying that God would wake me up in the morning, and then I would wake up thanking him for bringing me through the night. I would walk around every corner, in every field, at every moment looking for snakes and praying for protection. Everywhere and at all times I was aware of my need for him, and I lived in constant dependence upon him and in desperation for him.

I am convinced this is the way the Christian life is intended to be lived and our churches are intended to be led. Let's be honest. As long as church consists of normal routines and Christianity consists of nominal devotion with little risk, little sacrifice, and little abandonment, then we can do this on our own. But what happens when we give ourselves to something that is far greater than what we can accomplish on our own? What happens when we dare to believe that God desires to use every one of our lives and every one of our churches to bring about kingdom advancement to the ends of the earth? We will find ourselves around every corner and at every moment dependent on his power and desperate for his grace as we devote ourselves to his purpose.

GIVE GOD NO REST

Over the last couple of years, I have been convicted that prayer has been supplemental, not fundamental, in my life and in the church I lead. I began to ask myself, If someone were looking from the outside at the Church at Brook Hills, would they see a people desperate for the Spirit of God? Unfortunately, the clear answer to that question was no. So I began calling our faith family to pray and fast together, and now we take a Sunday during every quarter of the year to spend concentrated time in corporate prayer and fasting.

I realize that many churches here and around the world fast more intentionally and more frequently than this. One Sunday we were hosting some brothers and sisters from Kenya, and it happened to be a day we were fasting. I had lunch with them the next day as we broke our fast, and they asked if we fasted regularly as a church.

I said, "We are just beginning to do this, and many of our people are fasting for the first time in their lives, but we are learning, and we have a lot more to learn in the days ahead."

Then I asked, "What about you? Do you fast regularly in your church?"

A long pause ensued. They looked at one another, each waiting for the other to respond, and then one brother, Samuel, finally spoke up.

"In our church," he said, "we begin every year with a month-long fast."

Whether fasting for a day or for a month, it's healthy for the

church to corporately express our hunger for God. Isaiah's words
to the people of Israel have constructed the frame of our fasting at
Brook Hills.

> I have posted watchmen on your walls, O Jerusalem;
>   they will never be silent day or night.
> You who call on the LORD,
>   give yourselves no rest,
> and give him no rest till he establishes Jerusalem
>   and makes her the praise of the earth.[11]

I love a phrase in the second verse: "Give him no rest till…"
I want to be part of a people who are giving God no rest from our
praying and seeking after him. I want to be part of a people who
are calling on the Lord day and night, refusing to leave God alone
because we hunger for God's Word in our lives and God's power
in his church and God's glory in all nations.

I want to give God no rest until we experience the power and
the presence of God that we see in the church in Acts. One man
preaches, and more than three thousand people are cut to the heart
and saved. The Lord is adding daily to their number those being
saved. The lame are walking, and the blind are seeing. Thousands
are coming to Christ at great cost, yet they can't be kept from pro-
claiming the gospel. God is picking up people and putting them
in remote deserts to talk to people who are wondering about Jesus,
the number of disciples is growing rapidly, and the gospel is
spreading with power. I want to be part of a move of God like
that. Do you?

Do you and I want to see the power of God raining down on his church in inexplicable ways? Do you and I want to see the justice of God restored in his church so that we stop ignoring the poverty, disease, starvation, and sickness that are rampant around us? Do you and I want to see the love of God rescuing sinners from all walks of life and redeeming his children from every nation, tribe, tongue, and people? Then let us give God no rest from our praising, confessing, and interceding, and let us watch him unleash his people in his church for his purpose in the world.

"GOD DOES NOT NEED ME"

We are selfless followers of a self-centered God. We exist for the glory of God, and God exists for the glory of God. The ultimate key to joining together in radical obedience to Christ is found in fostering a humble view of ourselves and a high view of God in the church. For when we see ourselves as completely dependent, utterly desperate children of God who live exclusively for him, then we will give ourselves in total abandonment to him for his great purpose in the world: the declaration of his gospel and the demonstration of his glory to all the peoples of the earth.

Let me close this chapter by sharing a personal story that I am not proud of.

Years ago I was hiking and covertly distributing gospel literature in an area of East Asia where many unreached people groups live. During the hike I discovered why these people have been unreached for generations: they are physically difficult to reach. My party would hike for hours to get to a small village that was tucked into the crevice of a mountain. It was a long, grueling, and dangerous trip.

One night we stopped to set up camp while we still had a bit of daylight. So I wandered off on my own to the top of a hill where I could overlook the terrain we were traversing. As I sat there looking over the landscape and thinking about all we were doing to try to get the gospel to these people groups, a thought came to mind: *God must be really glad to have me on his team.*

It just so happened that I was holding a book by A. W. Tozer entitled *The Knowledge of the Holy.* I opened it to the chapter on the self-sufficiency of God, and these were the first words I read:

> Almighty God, just because He is almighty, needs no support. The picture of a nervous, ingratiating God fawning over men to win their favor is not a pleasant one; yet if we look at the popular conception of God that is precisely what we see. Twentieth-century Christianity has put God on charity. So lofty is our opinion of ourselves that we find it quite easy, not to say enjoyable, to believe that we are necessary to God....
>
> Probably the hardest thought of all for our natural egotism to entertain is that God does not need our help. We commonly represent Him as a busy, eager, somewhat frustrated Father hurrying about seeking help to carry out His benevolent plan to bring peace and salvation to the world....
>
> Too many missionary appeals are based upon this fancied frustration of Almighty God. An effective speaker

can easily excite pity in his hearers, not only for the hea-
then but for the God who has tried so hard and so long
to save them and has failed for want of support. I fear
that thousands of younger persons enter Christian service
from no higher motive than to help deliver God from the
embarrassing situation His love has gotten Him into and
His limited abilities seem unable to get Him out of. Add
to this a certain degree of commendable idealism and a
fair amount of compassion for the underprivileged and
you have the true drive behind much Christian activity
today.[12]

The only way my prideful heart could have more clearly heard a
message from God was if he had audibly spoken to me.

Humbled by the reality of a self-existent, self-sustaining, self-
sufficient God, I realized:

God does not need me.

God does not need my church.

God does not need you.

God does not need your church.

God does not need our conferences, conventions, plans, programs, budgets, buildings, or mission agencies.

The reality is that you and I, your church and my church, all
the structures we have constructed and all the stuff we have created could turn to dust, and God could still make a great name for
himself among the nations.

God does not involve us in his grand, global purpose because he needs us. He involves us in his grand, global purpose because he loves us.

So here we sit, with the gospel of God in our hearts, with the gift of God known as the church, and with a grand and gracious invitation from God to lock arms with one another in the passionate spread of his glory to the ends of the earth. Let's rise up together as selfless followers of a self-centered God, and let's live—and die—as though we believe our highest prize is his global praise.

CONCLUSION

How can we in the church best unleash the people of God in the Spirit of God with the Word of God for the glory of God in the world?

This question consumes me. I want my life and the church I am a part of to count for the mobilization of God's people and the completion of God's purpose. I join with others who, like you, don't want to miss out on the thrill of radical obedience to Christ in the world because I am busy maintaining business as usual in the church. I want to be a part of a community of faith that is enjoying the great pleasures of God in the context of abandonment to the global purpose of God.

Years ago Heather and I decided to begin praying a specific prayer together. We said to God, "Wherever you want us to go, whatever you want us to do, however you want us to live, we give our lives and our family for you to spend in making your gospel and your glory known to the ends of the earth, particularly among those who have never heard the gospel."

It was the everything-is-on-the-table moment in our marriage.

I sometimes wonder why God used that prayer to lead me to pastor a church in Birmingham, Alabama, where there is a myriad of other churches and multitudes of other Christians. And I'm not alone in thinking this. Last week a man from another church who is not a big fan of *Radical* said to me, "You just need to leave and go live in another country, and I'd be happy to help you get there."

Maybe the Lord *will* end up leading us to live overseas one day. Every time we commission a church-planting team to go into another part of the world, Heather and I put ourselves in front of the levee and ask God to sweep our current lives away if he so desires. But at this point, in his wisdom God has given me the privilege of pastoring an incredible people called the Church at Brook Hills. This church, like yours, is composed of wonderful men and women who have not been designed by God to waste their lives on good church activity devoid of great kingdom productivity. Instead, these men and women have been destined by God to spend their lives in the urgent task of announcing God's reign and advancing his kingdom to the ends of the earth.

We are constantly exploring what being radical together looks like in the context of our faith family. My intent in this book has not been to put forward Brook Hills as a perfect model. We are on a journey, and we have a long way to go as a church. More specifically, I have a long way to go as a pastor. My brothers and sisters have been patient with me as together we are discovering how to best share and spend our lives together for God's glory in the world.

Obviously, other churches are implementing obedience to

Christ and his purposes in the world in different ways. Small groups and churches, from Florida to California, are participating in variations of the Radical Experiment, a challenge with five steps that I proposed at the end of *Radical* (see www.radical experiment.org). Those steps include taking a year to pray for the entire world, read through the entire Word, sacrifice resources for a specific purpose, spend time in another context, and share life in a multiplying community.

Are these steps radical in and of themselves? For some, the answer has been yes. For others, the answer has been no. But for all, the aim has been to set our lives and our churches in motion by putting ourselves in positions where God can mold our hearts with his gracious Word for his glorious purpose.

The effect has been widespread. Men and women in the church are moving into high-risk areas in our cities and in other countries. Others are staying put and sacrificing earthly resources for eternal reward in their lives and their churches. Whether it is a mission church in El Salvador, a metropolitan church in London, a multiethnic church start in the northern United States, or a 150-year-old church in the South, communities of faith are experiencing the joy of deeper satisfaction in Christ through deeper surrender to Christ.

For example, one church took the Radical Experiment and adjusted its elements to create what they are calling the Kingdom Challenge. In their words, "The Kingdom Challenge is a strategy that challenges believers to obey Christ's command to deny self, take up our cross daily, and forsake all that we have to follow him in expanding his kingdom." They are "praying daily for unreached people groups (Luke 10:2); taking the gospel to those who have little or no access to it (Acts 1:8); discipling others in developing a biblical worldview (Matthew 28:19); meeting the physical and spiritual needs of the poor, orphaned, and widowed (James 1:27); and providing medical care for children who are susceptible to deadly diseases in poverty-stricken areas (Matthew 25:36, 40)."

As they call one another to selfless living and radical giving, they are sharing and showing the gospel locally in inner-city housing projects, mobile home communities, and residential rehab programs. Globally, they are partnering with churches in impoverished areas to provide clean water, orphan care, and ministry support for the sake of reaching unreached people with the gospel. One member of this church said, "Our God is sovereign, and we are trusting him to do great things in and through us. We want to be faithful to proclaim the gospel all around the world as we look forward to one day worshiping alongside every tribe and nation."

Who can imagine what might happen as communities of faith intentionally pray for the world, walk through the Word, sacrifice their resources, and spread the gospel in their neighborhoods and among the nations, particularly where the name of Jesus is not yet known? Regardless of whether or not a church goes through a specific variation of the Radical Experiment, what happens when steps similar to these become the new normal in the church? There is no end to the possibilities when God's people come together in absolute devotion to God's purpose.

Some may say, "Well, isn't all of this a bit extreme? Selling possessions and adopting children and adjusting lifestyles and going overseas. People might get carried away with all this talk about taking the gospel to the nations."

To this I say, so what? What if we do get carried away in taking the gospel to the nations? What will happen? The nations will end up being reached with the gospel, and then Jesus will come back. I think that's a reward worth the risk.

To return to imagery from the introduction, you and I find ourselves rushing down a mountain, our eyes opened to the gospel of Christ in his Word and our hearts longing for the glory of Christ in the world. We have been joined together in the church by God's grand design for a purpose that is far greater than any of us could imagine or achieve alone. So let's live radical together in eager anticipation of the day when we will see his face and, as a community encompassing every nation, tribe, tongue, and people, enjoy his beauty for all of eternity.

GOING FURTHER WITH RADICAL TOGETHER

A DISCUSSION GUIDE FOR SMALL GROUPS AND LEADERSHIP TEAMS

SIX SESSIONS

If *Radical Together* has struck a chord within you, then I encourage you to get together with a few other people whom you serve God alongside and talk about how to implement the six key ideas of this book in your church or ministry area.

Your group might be made up of pastors or other paid staff members. It might be made up of unpaid leaders in the church. It might be made up of people who have no specific role in church leadership but who want to be influencers for the kingdom. Regardless, the key is that you all have a passion for seeing God's people fulfill God's purpose within the context of the church.

The following sessions will guide you through discussion and planning about what you can do. As you meet together, keep in mind these guidelines:

- *Focus on yourself and the church or ministry area where you have responsibilities.* The point is not to criticize or interfere with others but to figure out what you can do to follow God better in the sphere where God has entrusted you with influence. As you pursue change, work within God-given authority structures.

- *Feel free to adapt the material for its best use in your particular group.* Depending on the makeup of your group and the type of issues you are facing, you may want to add or eliminate discussion questions or otherwise change the agenda to achieve what God is calling your group to do.

- *Be bold about God and humble about yourself.* God might have amazing things in store for you. Get ready for them! And remember that it's not because *you* have it all figured out but because *he* is in control.

Obviously, I don't know how abandonment to the purpose of God should play out in your life or church. I'm continually exploring what this looks like in the church I serve! But the Spirit of God is good. He desires the spread of the gospel and the declaration of God's glory among all peoples far more than we do. He will lead us. He will guide us. He will direct us as we put our lives and our churches on the table and ask him to use us to magnify his name by making disciples of all nations.

One final thing: When God does something exciting in your life and church, please share it with others at www.radical together.com. Together, we'll spur one another on in the church for God's purpose in the world.

—David Platt

PRIORITIZING KINGDOM
PRODUCTIVITY

KEY IDEA: ONE OF THE WORST ENEMIES OF CHRISTIANS CAN BE GOOD THINGS IN THE CHURCH.

We can easily deceive ourselves into thinking that dedication to church programs automatically equals devotion to kingdom purposes. We can fill our lives and our churches with *good* things that require our resources and *good* activities that demand our attention but are not ultimately *best* for the enjoyment of the gospel in our churches and the spread of the gospel in our communities. We must be willing to sacrifice good things in the church in order to experience the great things of God.

SCRIPTURAL PREPARATION

Read Philippians 3:4–16, a passage where Paul says that everything else is rubbish compared to knowing and conforming to Christ. His focus is laserlike: "One thing I do: Forgetting what is behind and straining toward what is ahead, I press on toward the goal to win the prize for which God has called me heavenward in Christ Jesus" (verses 13–14).

Then read Acts 20:22–24, where Paul describes how everything in his life is dedicated to one purpose: spreading the gospel to the ends of the earth. It is the only reason for which he has breath.

OPENING PRAYER: Pray for God to give your group laserlike focus on Christ and his purpose in the world. Ask God to give you new eyes to look at what you are doing in ministry, and ask him for a willing heart to put everything in your life and in the church on the table before him. Pray for him to reveal what he most wants you to spend your time and resources on.

GROUP DISCUSSION

Talk about your answers to the following questions and any others you believe would be helpful for your group. You might want to have your church mission statement, church budget, or similar documents available to review.

1. Considering the structure and activities of your church (or ministry area), in what ways might these things foster religious activity that results in little spiritual productivity?

2. What specific facets of your church or ministry area (programs, preferences, practices, traditions, facilities, and so on) are most difficult for you personally to put

on the table, and why? How do you think people in
your church would answer this question?

3. If your heart were to beat for the lost and the poor the
   way that God's does, how would that change how you
   are living personally? How would that change what
   your group is doing in the church?

4. What are you currently giving your time, energy, and
   resources to in the church that may be good but not
   best? How can you reorganize your lives and leadership
   around what is best?

5. If you were going to start a church (or ministry area)
   from scratch today, how would you structure it? How
   would you allocate your resources? What would your
   goals be?

IDEA BRAINSTORMING

Using a dry-erase board or a flip chart, create a list of ideas from
all group members in answer to these questions:

- What good things in your church (or ministry)
  might you need to abolish or alter in order to
  accomplish greater things for the glory of God?

- What greater things could you do for the glory of
  God with the time, energy, and resources you have
  in your church (or ministry)?

Remember, everything is on the table. So there's no need to evaluate ideas in any depth at this time. Just throw them out for consideration.

YOUR RESPONSE

Begin sorting through your ideas. Which ones spark broad interest within the group? Which ones can you get started on? If you do not have decision-making authority in your church, who might you talk to about them, and what might be some helpful and unifying ways to go about effecting these kinds of changes? Remember that people like change—until it affects them. So consider how best to shepherd the people you lead through any change you implement.

Create a list of three or more action steps. Identify who will do what and when. Plan for follow-up.

CLOSING PRAYER: Remember that we should never ask God to bless our plans but instead should ask God to help us fulfill his plans. So as you prepare to put into action what you think God is calling you to do, humbly invite him to shepherd you to do only what brings him glory. Continue praying to know his will better.

UNDERSTANDING

GRACE AND WORK

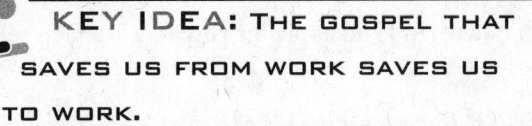

KEY IDEA: THE GOSPEL THAT
SAVES US FROM WORK SAVES US
TO WORK.

While we can never do enough to earn acceptance from God, Christ offers this acceptance as a gift when we trust in him. As we receive this gift, God equips and empowers us to serve him in all kinds of ways. Consequently, we must avoid becoming churches full of people who are continually working hard to earn the approval of God while eventually wearing out in our assignment from God. And we must also avoid becoming churches full of people who are constantly defending the gospel while rarely demonstrating it.

SCRIPTURAL PREPARATION

Read Ephesians 2:1–10 aloud in your group. Notice especially how "works" (in verse 9) are incapable of achieving our salvation, yet "works" (verse 10) were God's plan for us from eternity past. To underscore the necessity of good works in response to God's grace in our lives, read James 2:14–26. A faith without deeds is no faith at all.

OPENING PRAYER: Begin your prayer time with silent confession, each group member (as needed) asking forgiveness from God for either devaluing God's grace or devaluing good works. Conclude by praying for God to help the group members both understand and apply his gospel.

GROUP DISCUSSION

Talk over your answers to the following questions and any others that you believe would be helpful for your group. Begin by reviewing the description of Andy and Ashley at the beginning of chapter 2.

1. Who are you more like: Andy or Ashley?
   - If you are more like Andy, what steps can you take to grow in your faith in a way that bears fruit in your life, particularly in your love for people in need?
   - If you are more like Ashley, what steps can you take to rest continually in the gospel and not see work as your attempt to find favor with God?

2. Thinking about the Andys and Ashleys in your church (or ministry), how can you best shepherd each kind of person to follow radically after Christ?

3. What is the gospel, and how does the gospel practically affect your life? What would be your answers to the following questions?

   - How can I be saved?

   - How can I become holy?

   - How can I be sure of my salvation?

4. How can you guard against guilt as a motivation in the church? How can you practically make the gospel your motivation in the church?

5. Thinking about the ministry you have responsibility for, what kind of imbalance do you see in it with regard to grace and works?

6. What benefits can accrue when you get the gospel (both the "saves us from work" and the "saves us to work" parts) right?

IDEA BRAINSTORMING

Once more, remember what the gospel teaches: we are to trust in God's grace alone to make us acceptable before God *and at the same time* to pursue good works for God's glory with everything we have. With that in mind, create a list of ideas from all the group members in answer to the following questions:

- What specific actions could you take to correct misunderstandings of the gospel in your church (or ministry)?
- What specific actions could you take to foster a healthy understanding of the gospel in your church (or ministry) in the future?

YOUR RESPONSE

Looking at your list from the idea brainstorming, what specific ideas do you want to act on? Flesh out those ideas as necessary to come up with an effective action plan.

Keep in mind that this is not about condemning anyone. This is about making a fresh start to live in God's grace and fulfill his plan for our lives. Recovering a fully rounded biblical understanding of God's grace in the gospel is a wonderfully freeing experience for all of us Andys and Ashleys!

CLOSING PRAYER: Ask God to use your group powerfully in making your church a more fully gospel-formed body for his glory.

BASING EVERYTHING

ON THE BIBLE

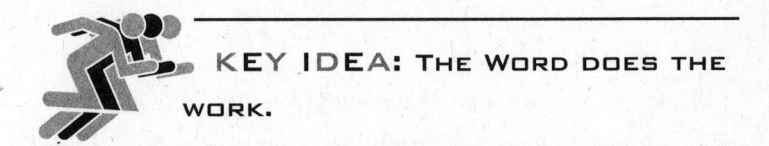

KEY IDEA: THE WORD DOES THE
WORK.

When the words of mere humans drive how and where we are going, we will get nowhere. But when we unchain the power of God's Word in the church, it will unleash the potential of God's people in the world. So if we want to make God's glory known in the world, then we must make the teaching of God's Word central in the church. And as we hold fast to God's Word, we can trust that he will ultimately use it to accomplish his intended, eternal, global purpose.

SCRIPTURAL PREPARATION

Do we want to be fruitful for God? John 15:1–8 shows us how. Read this passage, and notice the repeated emphasis on remaining in Christ and his teachings. Indeed, remaining in the whole Word of God is the key to being productive for God both as individuals and as a church.

OPENING PRAYER: Together, thank God for the precious gift of his Word. Perhaps some of your group can use memorized phrases from Scripture in praying God's Word back to him. Commit yourselves to putting the Bible before any man-made notions that would contradict it. Ask for God's help in making Scripture the basis of all you do in his service.

GROUP DISCUSSION

Talk over your answers to the following questions and any others that you believe would be helpful for your group. Have Bibles available so that group members can read passages if they want.

1. What texts in God's Word are particularly foundational for your personal life? For your church (or ministry)?

2. How have you seen human words maximized and God's Word minimized in some churches? What about your church? What about your leadership?

3. How does finding your authority in God's Word change your leadership among God's people?

4. What are some ways you are seeing God's Word at work in your church?

5. How are you demonstrating trust in the sufficiency of God's Word in your personal life and leadership? What practical steps can your church take to demonstrate greater trust in the sufficiency of God's Word?

6. How well is your church's theology aligned with the Bible? How well is your church's methodology aligned with the Bible?

IDEA BRAINSTORMING

Using a dry-erase board or a flip chart, draw two columns. Label the left-hand column "In God's Word" and the right-hand column "Not in God's Word." In the left-hand column, list things you do in your church or ministry that are directly commanded in God's Word. In the right-hand column, list things you do that are not directly commanded in God's Word.

Of course, those things that are not directly commanded in God's Word are not necessarily bad. But as chapter 1 says, some of them may be good things that we need to give up in order to pursue God's best, and God's best is commanded in his Word.

Keeping your two-column chart visible as a reference, create a separate list of responses to the following questions:

- How can you give less time to things that are not commanded in God's Word and more time to things that are commanded in God's Word?

- What specific texts of Scripture will guide planning and strategizing in your church (or ministry) in the future?

YOUR RESPONSE

When group members have run out of responses to the brain-storming questions above, begin sorting through options to find ideas your group wants to act upon. Settle on a specific plan that you can carry out.

CLOSING PRAYER: Confess to God your trust in his Word, and commit to conform your church (or ministry) more and more to his Word.

MAKING DISCIPLES

KEY IDEA: BUILDING THE RIGHT
CHURCH DEPENDS ON USING ALL THE
WRONG PEOPLE.

Too often churches in America focus on *performances, places, programs,* and *professionals.* But if the spread of the gospel is dependent on these things, we will never reach the ends of the earth. What's missing here is *people.* In Jesus' simple command to "make disciples," he has invited every one of his followers to share his life with others in a sacrificial, intentional, global effort to multiply the gospel through others. This includes not just the "right" people (our most effective communicators, most brilliant organizers, and most talented leaders and artists) but also the "wrong" people (those who are the least effective, brilliant, or talented in the church).

SCRIPTURAL PREPARATION

In 1 Corinthians 3:16, Paul asks, "Don't you know that you yourselves are God's temple and that God's Spirit lives in you?" The answer to that question for many Christians today, sadly, is no. Theoretically, we get it. But practically, in our churches and ministries, we may be relying on anything but God's Spirit in every one of our brothers and sisters to fulfill God's plan in the world.

Where does the biblical perspective on the church leave church leaders? Read Ephesians 4:11–16 for the leaders' roles as preparers of others for service as the church grows up in the image of Christ.

OPENING PRAYER: Together, pray for God's grace to adjust fully to the mind-set that church leaders are not to be stars but humble equippers of others to do ministry. Pray for growth in the maturity of your church or ministry, asking especially that the people you serve will increasingly and more clearly reflect Christ to the world.

GROUP DISCUSSION

Talk over your answers to the following questions and any others that you believe would be helpful for your group. Keep in mind that disciple making is the goal.

1. In what ways has your church (or ministry) become unhealthily dependent

    • on performances?

    • on places?

    • on programs?

    • on professionals?

2. How might your church look different if every member (even the "wrong" ones) were fully involved in serving Christ?

3. Who is the most recent person you had the opportunity to lead to Christ and then disciple and who is now discipling others? What did you learn in this process of making disciples?

4. What are the most significant obstacles you face personally when it comes to prioritizing disciple making? How can you overcome these obstacles?

5. What are the most significant obstacles your church (or ministry) faces when it comes to prioritizing disciple making? How can you help overcome these obstacles?

6. How can you best lead your church (or ministry) to reproduce disciple makers?

IDEA BRAINSTORMING

Dream together for a while about what your church or ministry might look like if it more fully adhered to Christ's simple yet radical plan for spreading the gospel by making disciples. Write down the group members' ideas about the following questions:

- How can you become less dependent on performances? (That is, how can you foster a participant's approach to church more than a spectator's approach?)

- How can you spend fewer resources on places? (Discuss what alternatives there might be to constructing bigger buildings, adding more space, and using multitudes of resources on building places instead of people.)

- How can you become less focused on programs? (How can you lead your church to shift from organizing ministry for people to mobilizing people for ministry?)

- How can you become less dependent on professionals? (Discuss ways that leadership can focus more on equipping members in the church as well as ways that members can focus more on involvement in ministry in the church.)

- What would a disciple-making plan look like for your church or ministry? (How would people share their time, God's Word, and the gospel with others? How would people help others grow in Christ? How would they equip people to invest in yet other people?)

YOUR RESPONSE

Focusing especially on the last question in your brainstorming time, agree on a disciple-making plan that you will promote for your church or ministry. What is the best way to get started on it? (And remember, each of you should be doing it too!)

CLOSING PRAYER: Thank God for those who have graciously invested the gospel in you. Ask his help to fulfill the calling not only to be a disciple maker yourself but also to share the vision of disciple making with others.

REACHING THE

UNREACHED

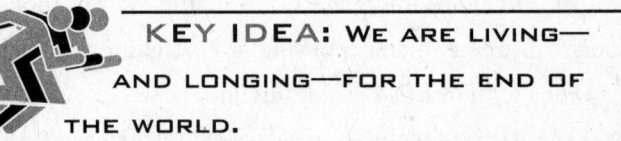

KEY IDEA: WE ARE LIVING—AND LONGING—FOR THE END OF THE WORLD.

Jesus has called, commissioned, and commanded each of us as Christians to give ourselves to the spread of his gospel in every part of the earth. All nations, all tribes, all language groups, and all peoples will one day hear this news, and then the end will come. As a result, every church that passionately loves the gospel of Christ and patiently longs for the coming of Christ will purposefully live for the glory of Christ among those who have never heard his name.

SCRIPTURAL PREPARATION

Have three members of your group read

- the command to take the gospel to all people groups (Matthew 28:16–20);
- a promise of what will happen when all people groups are finally reached (Matthew 24:14);

- a vision of the glorious fulfillment of that promise
  (Revelation 7:9–10).

If this isn't something to live for, what is?

OPENING PRAYER: Before beginning to pray, pause and consider what your life would be like if you had never heard the gospel. After a few moments of meditating on this thought, ask God to give every member of your group a glimpse of his love and yearning for unreached peoples around the world. Ask him to use you as catalysts for the strategic spread of the gospel to the ends of the earth.

GROUP DISCUSSION

Talk over your answers to the following questions and any others that you believe would be helpful for your group. You might wish to have a tool like *Operation World* available as a reference.

1. How is your life as a Christian impacting unreached people with the gospel? How is your leadership in the church impacting unreached people with the gospel?

2. In what ways is your church being obedient to Jesus' command to make disciples of all nations? In what ways is your church being disobedient to this command?

3. How can you lead your church (or ministry) to prioritize taking the gospel to unreached peoples?

4. What obstacles might you face inside the church if you lead your church to focus on unreached peoples? How can you best address those obstacles?

5. What obstacles might you face outside the church if you lead your church to focus on unreached peoples? How can you best address those obstacles?

IDEA BRAINSTORMING

Create a list of ideas in response to the following questions:

- How can you intentionally mobilize people in your church to reach unreached people groups with the gospel?
- How can you intentionally reach out to people from other countries who are currently living in your community?

YOUR RESPONSE

Based upon your brainstorming, what specific steps could your group take action on immediately? Agree to work together as a team to pursue these steps, carry out additional research and planning, and keep encouraging one another. (Maybe you'll even want to go overseas soon!)

CLOSING PRAYER: Praise God for his glorious plan to rescue people from every nation, tribe, and language to worship him together. And thank him for letting you be a part of that plan.

DESIRING GOD'S GLORY

KEY IDEA: WE ARE SELFLESS FOLLOWERS OF A SELF-CENTERED GOD.

We exist for the glory of God, and God exists for the glory of God. The ultimate key to joining together in radical obedience to Christ is found in fostering a humble view of ourselves and a high view of God in the church. For when we see ourselves as completely dependent, utterly desperate children of God who live exclusively for him, then we will give ourselves in total abandonment to him for his great purpose in the world: the declaration of his gospel and the demonstration of his glory to all the peoples of the earth.

SCRIPTURAL PREPARATION

Too often we are self-centered followers of a selfless god we have invented. We think God exists to serve and exalt us, instead of the other way around. In this we could not be more wrong.

Are we to seek comfort for ourselves? No. We are to accept a cross. Read Matthew 10:37–39.

Does God do great things in us or through us because we

deserve them? No. He does great things in us and through us to exalt his own holy name. Read Ezekiel 36:22–23.

OPENING PRAYER: Ask God's forgiveness for the times you have given in to the human tendency to make yourself the center of the universe. Ask also that he would make you and all the members of your group agents for spreading the vision of making God's glory the highest priority.

GROUP DISCUSSION

Talk over your answers to the following questions and any others that you believe would be helpful for your group.

1. What does it mean in your life for you to die to yourself? What does this mean in your leadership?

2. How does God's centering around himself change the way you live? How does this change the way you lead?

3. What are you leading in your church (or ministry) right now that absolutely cannot be accomplished apart from the supernatural power of God?

4. In what ways is your church selflessly following a self-centered God?

5. In what ways is your church perhaps following a selfless god in a self-centered fashion?

6. Is prayer fundamental or supplemental in your life? What about in your leadership? What about in your church?

7. What would the members of your church say is the vision of your church? What would you want them to say?

IDEA BRAINSTORMING

List the group's suggested answers to these questions:

- How can you lead your church (or ministry) to have a unified vision built around exalting the glory of God?
- How can you lead your church (or ministry) to become more desperate for and dependent on the power of God in prayer?

YOUR RESPONSE

As you have done with previous action plans, come up with specific steps your group will take to implement the best ideas for helping your church or ministry to put its highest priority on seeking the glory of God.

Review action plans from past sessions and evaluate where they stand. What more do you need to do to keep making progress on them?

Talk about if and how you want to keep working together on the issues raised in *Radical Together.*

CLOSING PRAYER: Spend time praising and worshiping almighty God simply for who he is.

ACKNOWLEDGMENTS

This work is the fruit of God's grace expressed to me in innumerable ways.

I am indebted to the wonderful team at Multnomah, to Eric for his invaluable wisdom and to Dave for his masterful skill as an editor and his gracious encouragement as a friend.

I am indebted to Sealy, whose trusted counsel and tireless service are a clear testimony of his love for Christ and the church.

I am indebted to church leaders around the world who have taught me—and shown me—the beauty of the body of Christ and the primacy of the local church. To Charles in East Asia, Chris in Southeast Asia, Ramesh in South Asia, Jeffries in Africa, Dominic in Latin America, and Mark in North America, I am deeply grateful for your leadership in the church and your influence in my life.

I am indebted to the elders, staff, and members of the Church at Brook Hills. Your patience with me is remarkable evidence of God's mercy to me, and I am honored to be your pastor. I love you, church.

I am indebted to my family in ways that words could never express. Caleb and Joshua, thank you for loving your daddy the way you do. Heather, thank you for tenderly enduring all that is involved in having me as your husband—and you alone know all that entails! You are my beautiful bride and best friend, and this book is yet more evidence of your desire to give your life for the glory of Christ in all nations.

May God's grace to me be to great effect for him (John 3:30).

NOTES

INTRODUCTION

1. Matthew 19:30; Luke 9:48; Matthew 10:39.
2. In the fall of 2010, I taught a doctrinal study on the body of Christ at Brook Hills during our Secret Church experience. This five-hour teaching covers basic ecclesiology, and it is available at www.secretchurch.org. In the back of the listening guide for this study (which you can download from the Secret Church Web site), I provide a bibliography of resources for further study on the doctrine of the church. In addition, I highly recommend Mark Dever, *Nine Marks of a Healthy Church* (Wheaton, IL: Crossway, 2004) and the resources available at www.9marks.org.
3. Leviticus 26:12; Romans 12:5; 1 Peter 2:9; Ephesians 3:10.

CHAPTER 1: TYRANNY OF THE GOOD

1. Luke 14:33; 9:23.
2. Mark 7:8.
3. James 2:14–17.
4. "Giving Research," Empty Tomb, www.emptytomb.org/fig1_07 .html; John Ronsvalle and Sylvia Ronsvalle, *The State of Church Giving Through 2003,* 15th ed. (Champaign, IL: Empty Tomb, 2005), 104.

CHAPTER 2: THE GOSPEL MISUNDERSTOOD

1. Ephesians 2:8–10; James 2; 1 John 3:16–18.
2. Romans 4; Galatians 3.

3. Ephesians 2:8–9.

4. 1 Thessalonians 1:3; 2 Thessalonians 1:11; Galatians 5:6.

5. Matthew 7:15–20; Genesis 15:1–6; 22:1–9; James 2:20–24; Joshua 2; James 2:25–26; 1 Corinthians 15:10; Colossians 1:27–29.

6. James 2:23; John 3:1–21; 15:1–17.

7. 1 Corinthians 15:1–11; Ephesians 2:1–10.

8. James 1:27.

CHAPTER 3: GOD IS SAYING SOMETHING

1. Matthew 28:20; 1 Timothy 3:2.

2. John 15:5, 7–8.

3. I am grateful to John Piper for encouraging me to pray this prayer in light of Brainerd's example. John Piper, "Making a Difference by Fire," Desiring God, October 2, 1989, www .desiringgod.org/resource-library/taste-see-articles/making-a-difference-by-fire.

4. 1 Kings 3:7.

5. 2 Timothy 3:10–4:5.

6. Walter C. Kaiser Jr., "The Crisis in Expository Preaching Today," *Preaching* (September–October 1995): 6, www .preaching.com/resources/articles/11565532/page-2/.

7. Genesis 19:30–38; Numbers 25:1–9; Ruth 1–4; Matthew 1:1–17.

8. 1 Corinthians 10:31.

9. Job 42:2; Isaiah 46:9–11; 55:10–11.

10. John 15:18.

11. Isaiah 55:10–11.

CHAPTER 4: THE GENIUS OF WRONG

1. David Platt, *Radical: Taking Back Your Faith from the American Dream* (Colorado Springs: Multnomah, 2010), 48–50.

2. Hebrews 10:24–25.

3. Acts 4:32–35; 2 Corinthians 8–9.

4. Acts 7:48.

5. Matthew 27:51.

6. 1 Corinthians 3:16; 6:18–20.

7. 1 Corinthians 7:32–34.

8. Acts 1:8; 2:17–18; Joel 2:28–29.

9. John 14:12.

10. 1 Timothy 5:17–18; 1 Corinthians 9:8–18; 1 Timothy 3:2–3, 8.

11. Ephesians 4:12.

12. Ephesians 4:16.

13. You can find a template for our new member disciple-making plans on our church's Web site, www.brookhills.org/new/impact .html. Click on "Get Homework Assignment #3."

14. Quoted in Paul Hattaway, Brother Yun, Peter Xu Yongze, and Enoch Wang, *Back to Jerusalem: Three Chinese House Church Leaders Share Their Vision to Complete the Great Commission* (Waynesboro, GA: Gabriel Publishing, 2003), 64, 108, 133–34.

15. Matthew 24:14; Revelation 7:9–10; Romans 10:13–15.

CHAPTER 5: OUR UNMISTAKABLE TASK

1. George Eldon Ladd, *The Gospel of the Kingdom: Scriptural Studies in the Kingdom of God* (Grand Rapids: Eerdmans, 1959), 123.

2. Matthew 28:19.

3. Blessing on Israel (Genesis 12:1–3; 28:14); out of slavery (Deuteronomy 4:5–6; 1 Kings 4:34); exile (Ezekiel 36:22–23; Daniel 3:29; 6:26); Jesus' command to preach (Luke 24:47; see also Acts 1:8); story of the church (Acts 26:16–18; 28:28); consuming ambitions (Romans 15:20).

4. Revelation 7:9–10; see also 5:9–10.

5. Revelation 22:20.

6. Matthew 24:36.

7. Ladd, *The Gospel of the Kingdom,* 137.

8. Matthew 24:9.

9. Revelation 12:11.

10. Acts 17:6, KJV.

CHAPTER 6: THE GOD WHO EXALTS GOD

1. Free to spend our lives however he pleases (Matthew 10:37–39; Luke 9:57–62; 14:25–33); declares his own glory (Isaiah 40; Psalm 96); displays his own glory (Psalm 19:1–4; 148–150); worthy of all exaltation (Revelation 19:1–10); worthy of all praise from all peoples (Ezekiel 36:22–23).

2. KJV.

3. Romans 3:11.

4. John 4:23.

5. 1 Corinthians 14:24–25.

6. Quoted in Courtney Anderson, *To the Golden Shore: The Life of Adoniram Judson* (Valley Forge, PA: Judson, 1987), 83.

7. Acts 1:14; 2:42; 6:4.

8. Acts 2 as a result of Acts 1; 4:4 as a result of 3:1; 4:31 as a result of 4:29; 6:7 as a result of 6:3–4; 8:1–4 as a result of 7:59–60;

9:18 as a result of 9:13; 10:47–48 as a result of 10:9; 16:33 as a result of 16:25.

9. Acts 4:33.

10. Acts 6:8; 11:23; 13:43; 14:3, 26; 15:11, 40; 18:27; 20:24, 32.

11. Isaiah 62:6–7.

12. A. W. Tozer, *The Knowledge of the Holy: The Attributes of God; Their Meaning in the Christian Life* (New York: Harper, 1961), 34.

ABOUT THE AUTHOR

DR. DAVID PLATT is the author of the *New York Times* best-selling book *Radical*. He is also lead pastor of the Church at Brook Hills in Birmingham, Alabama.

David's first love in ministry is multiplying the gospel by making disciples. "I believe that God has uniquely created every one of his people to impact the world," he says. "God is in the business of blessing his people so that his ways and his salvation might be made known among all peoples." To this end, David has traveled throughout the United States and around the world, teaching the Bible and training church leaders.

David has earned two undergraduate degrees from the University of Georgia and three advanced degrees, including a doctor of philosophy from New Orleans Baptist Theological Seminary. Prior to coming to Brook Hills, he served the seminary as dean of chapel and assistant professor of expository preaching and apologetics and was on staff at Edgewater Baptist Church in New Orleans.

David and his wife, Heather, are Atlanta natives who made their home in New Orleans until they were displaced by Hurricane Katrina. They live with their family in Birmingham.

To find out more about David Platt, go to www.disciple makingintl.org.

Deepen Your Understanding

with these additional resources

"Do you believe that Jesus is worth abandoning everything for?"

In *Radical*, David Platt invites you to encounter what Jesus actually said about being his disciple, and then obey what you have heard. He challenges you to consider with an open heart how we have manipulated a God-centered gospel to fit our human-centered preferences. Then he proposes a radical response: live the gospel in ways that are true, filled with promise, and ultimately world changing.

In this brief companion booklet, David Platt reveals what can happen in the world when we exchange our convenient beliefs for authentic discipleship.

Available as a 10-pack.

Find information, tools for individual application, church resources, and video at **RadicalTheBook.com**.

 MULTNOMAH BOOKS
www.waterbrookmultnomah.com

Radical: The Bible Study

Powerful truths to share with your church, Sunday school class, or small group.

Order at www.lifebiblestudy.com/radical or call 877.265.1605

Brought to you by LifeBibleStudy®